11-14-72

Reforms in the Soviet and Eastern European Economies

Reforms in the Soviet and Eastern European Economies

Edited by

L.A.D. Dellin
University of Vermont

Hermann Gross
Munich University

Lexington Books
D.C. Heath and Company
Lexington, Massachusetts
Toronto   London

Contents

vi

Preface

The present volume has its origins in an international symposium sponsored by the German learned society "Studiengesellschaft fuer Fragen mittel-und osteuropaeischer Partnerschaft" in Bonn. Devoted to "Economic Reforms in Eastern Europe–Congruence of the Economic Systems?," the symposium's proceedings were first published in German under the title *Osteuropa-Wirtschaftsreformen* (Bonn: Atlantic Forum 1970) and under the editorship of the German host, Hermann Gross.

The publication met with unusual interest, which might have been due as much to the topic as to the composition of the panel: This was Ota Sik's first lengthy public appearance following the Soviet-sponsored intervention in Czechoslovakia; Alec Nove needs no introduction as an authority on the Soviet economy, nor does Michael Gamarnikow or Willy Linder–the economics editor of the *Neue Zuercher Zeitung* and lecturer at Zuerich University–as authorities on Eastern European economics. German scholars–from the dean of Soviet and East European studies, Karl C. Thalheim of Berlin, to the young specialists of the Munich University Institute of Southeast European Economics, Johann Hawlowitsch and Claus D. Rohleder–provide the European tradition. The paper on the reforms of a little known country, Bulgaria, presented by the American editor of this volume, was published in an abbreviated form in *Problems of Communism* (September-October 1970). All in all, we have an unusual combination of panelists from both sides of the Atlantic, bringing different backgrounds, training, and experience to the discussion of a timely problem.

These remarks explain much of the reason for presenting the papers to the English-readers. The unavoidable passage of time has done little if any damage; it has happily confirmed the findings of the authors and has permitted not only some updating, wherever necessary, but also the closing of some gaps in the German edition. Thus, the omission of a paper on Poland has been remedied by a new article by Michael Gamarnikow, and an epilogue has attempted to provide some missing links and pave the way for the consideration of new problems connected with and resulting from our earlier assessment of East European economic reforms, problems such as the difference between reform plans and their implementation, the role of foreign trade, and the search for a new typology of Communist economic systems. Some of these matters were raised at a subsequent international meeting, the Sixth International Conference, organized jointly by the same German sponsor and its American associate, the Conference on European Problems (which superseded the Foundation for Foreign Affairs). Its proceedings have been published in a German volume edited by Alfred Domes and entitled *Reformen und Dogmen in Osteuropa* (Reforms and Dogmas in Eastern Europe) (Cologne: Wissenschaft und Politik, 1971). The lack of a separate paper on Eastern Germany has been at least partially remedied by repeated references to East German reforms in the concluding paper by Karl. C. Thalheim. Albania has yet to develop reform concepts, let alone implement any reform worth discussing. Finally, in lieu of a bibliography, the epilogue provides extensive footnote references of major recent works on economic reforms.

Any paraphrasing of the individual contributions in a preface would only adulterate their value. The editors simply wish to express their appreciation to the authors for their confidence. Appreciation is also due the German publisher and his American counterpart, especially Mr. Geoffrey S. Gunn, Director, Heath Lexington Books. Mr. Gunn is familiar with European scholarship at first hand, and he enthusiastically welcomed the opportunity to present the efforts of an international panel to the English-speaking reader. Special thanks are due all those who participated in the various stages in the preparation of the book, especially the staff of the Center for Area and International Studies of the University of Vermont.

The importance of the topic—reforms in planned economies—should be self-evident, especially in countries with communist party regimes, where the dividing line between economics and politics is hazy at best, and where the potential spill-over effect between the two may prove to be of cardinal significance for the future development of "communism." We hope, therefore, that the current volume will be useful to students of comparative economics and also of politics, and especially to students concentrating on the Soviet Union and Eastern Europe.

L.A.D. Dellin
University of Vermont

Hermann Gross
Munich University

May 1972

**Reforms in the Soviet
and Eastern European
Economies**

1 Introduction: Economics and Politics

Michael Gamarnikow

I

It is one of the basic tenets of the orthodox Marxist faith that the political superstructure of a given society is determined by the institutional forms of its economic base. A stable superstructure presupposes full harmony between the prevailing economic and social relations and the corresponding political system. Thus, the totalitarian power structure of the traditional orthodox communist state was, indeed, perfectly coordinated with the centralized institutions of a command economy and its arbitrary operational patterns. But the gradual implementation of pragmatic reforms tends to destroy this institutional equilibrium between the economic base and its political superstructure. The essence of all economic reform programs (regardless of the actual model adopted) is a far-reaching decentralization of economic decision-making and a substitution of material incentives and a (restricted) market mechanism for direct controls and arbitrary directives. Clearly, such qualitative changes in the economic sector could not fail to undermine the political power structure in the country affected.

As things stand now, the real issue is not whether the impact of economic reforms will result in really substantive changes in the totalitarian political system of the orthodox communist state, but how far this process will be allowed to go. Can one expect the dictatorship of the proletariat to evolve gradually into some specific form of pluralistic social democracy? Will any communist party once again make a genuine effort to build "socialism with a human face," and if so, can it get away with it? Today, with the Czechoslovak experience still rather fresh in our minds, one may be inclined, perhaps, to be skeptical. But is this skepticism really justified—especially in the long run?

It is not yet possible to unravel the complex motives that prompted the decision to invade Czechoslovakia. There can be little question, however, that one of the primary objectives of this armed intervention was to curtail the Dubcek regime's program of economic reforms because of its frank reliance on concomitant political liberalization.

If this assumption is correct—and there is a wealth of circumstantial evidence to support it—then the Czechoslovak precedent would seem to raise a serious question as to the future prospects of economic reform throughout the whole of Eastern Europe. What is at stake is not necessarily the process of economic change, in the limited sense of more rational and pragmatic methods of planning and management, but the broader impetus to bring about those qualitative changes in the orthodox power structure that seem absolutely necessary if the economic reforms are to succeed.

Despite a veritable barrage of propaganda directed some time ago against the "revisionist concepts" of Czechoslovakia's reform program, as well as against the Yugoslav economic model, it does not seem likely that the reformist trend throughout the Moscow bloc will be abruptly reversed or abandoned, although it may be temporarily slowed down. Even in Czechoslovakia, it is entirely possible that the essential vestiges of economic reform will still be salvaged, except for predictable changes in the highly sensitive sectors of foreign trade relations, import of capital, and direct workers' control. In Hungary, where the invasion of Czechoslovakia sparked a great deal of public anxiety about the future of the Hungarian economic model, the ruling elite has repeatedly confirmed its determination to proceed with the implementation of economic reforms.[1] There has also been no real evidence that the rest of the Moscow bloc intends to revise, let alone cancel, its economic reform programs. In short, the real bone of contention—both from the ideological and the political point of view—is not so much economic reform as its political implications.

It has long been openly admitted by the more perceptive Marxist scholars that economic reforms are bound, at least in the long run, to undermine the monopoly of power that every ruling communist party has so far enjoyed. "If we are today about to carry out very significant changes in the system of economic management," argued a Czechoslovak social scientist, months before the ouster of Novotny, "then obviously sooner or later these changes will have to find reflection in our political system as well."[2] As noted, Marxist doctrine is rooted in the belief that meaningful changes in the economic base of any society must have a profound impact on its political superstructure. Considering the relatively limited scope of even the most advanced economic reforms now being implemented throughout Eastern Europe, one would be certainly far too optimistic to expect those countries to evolve toward some form of integral democracy. However, since the new economic model does require a definite sense of active participation at all social levels, one can certainly hope for a gradual evolution into something that may be loosely defined as a participatory semi-authoritarian system.

Probably neither the dogmatists nor the reformers would deny that the monocentric methods of planning and management developed under Stalin were fully consistent with the traditional communist political power structure, based on the dictatorship of the Party elite. Within the framework of this system, the ruling oligarchy combined its monopoly of political power with full control over all essential economic decision-making. Thus the party establishment was able to predetermine economic priorities and totally subordinate economic development of the country to its doctrinal and political objectives. At the same time, the centralized command economy permitted the ruling elite to grant economic privileges to the huge bureaucratic-administrative apparatus, which has been the backbone of the system for many decades and which shaped this system in such a way that it evolved into a faithful reflection of its own bureaucratic mentality.

A pragmatic economic model was completely alien to such a power structure. One could easily predict that the *modus operandi* of the new economic system was bound, in the long run, to undermine the entire economic base of the monopoly of political power. For there was a very strong probability that a more participatory economic model would create a number of special interest groups, some of which might even evolve into new elites with powerful vested interests of their own. Such elites could then become real contenders for political power. Thus, it is very pertinent to ask the question: Why have the ruling oligarchies in Eastern Europe (and in the Soviet Union as well) embarked upon the road of economic reforms?

Before answering this question in terms of objective economic conditions (which, in fact, left the ruling elites with no option but to introduce meaningful changes into the existing system of planning and management), it might perhaps be useful to put the history of economic reforms in proper perspective.

The economic reform movement may properly be regarded as the second stage in the process of dismantling certain instruments of the monopoly of power considered essential for the Stalinist type of ultra-centralized, single-party dictatorship—the second stage in the process of de-Stalinization.

The first stage, involving essentially the abolition of terror and the curtailment of the powers of the secret police, had little direct impact on the economic system as such. All the really significant changes were largely political in character and their main effects confined to the administrative apparatus and lower rungs of the party establishment. Although at this stage some important concessions were also made to the population at large, the gist of early de-Stalinization was to establish a sort of personal security charter for party members, so long as they did not actively oppose the ruling oligarchy and its established policies.

This personal security charter was an essential element in the process of re-establishing the supremacy of the party leadership over the secret police, which was the basic objective of the initial stage of de-Stalinization. And the primary requirement for this was abolishing the system of terror. In a sense, all the concessions granted to (or sometimes usurped by) the population at large were really incidental to the basic objective of curbing the arbitrary powers of the secret police. In the course of this first stage of de-Stalinization, all Moscow bloc countries were compelled to purge some of the most compromised members of their ruling elites and security apparatus, and to rehabilitate many victims of the so-called cult of personality.

But the fact remains that neither the fragmentary purges at the top nor the transfers and dismissals of the most compromised people in the secret police apparatus, nor even the substantive, though secondary, concessions granted to the population at large, have really shaken the political structure of the traditional communist state. Subsequent experience has shown that such changes as occurred in the initial stage of de-Stalinization could easily be contained within a full-scale monopoly of power exercized by the "vanguard of the proletariat." And, as we have seen in Poland and in Czechoslovakia, whenever the impetus of de-Stalinization began to slacken off, the ruling oligarchy could easily reassert its administrative muscle.

Economic reforms mark a qualitatively different stage of the process of de-Stalinization. The impulsion toward a new system of planning and management, especially toward a new model of a more advanced type, presages an inexorable change in the existing balance of political power. The crux of all proposed reform blueprints, regardless of their degree of departure from the old system of arbitrary controls, has been the gradual transfer of decision-making power (at least in the field of micro-economics) from the party establishment and the central administrative apparatus to the new managerial class, and, in time (at least in theory), through the mechanism of the market, to the consumer. Such a transfer of economic prerogatives must inevitably weaken the position of both the party and the bureaucracy, since it strikes at the economic roots of their political power. It is also bound to put into focus the conflict among interest groups and strengthen the relative position of the "technocrats," who can be expected to assume increasing responsibility for economic decision-making under the new reform programs.

The resulting contradictions between the vested interests of the incumbent ruling elites and those who are bound to be the main beneficiaries of the new system of planning and management are likely to result in bitter political infighting (such as preceded the fall of Novotny in Czechoslovakia). This stage is likely to be reached when the ideological protagonists of the new economic model, as well as those who are likely to benefit from its fuller implementation, begin to realize that the new system cannot become fully effective without a significant degree of political democratization along pluralistic lines.

Changes in economic thinking and their impact on the intellectual elite cannot fail to weaken seriously the ideological basis of orthodox Marxism-Leninism, which has been the theoretical mainstay of the whole system of the dictatorship of the proletariat. *Economic empiricism must bring about political pragmatism, since in any Marxist system politics and economics are inseparably linked.*

There were other reasons why economic reforms emerged as the next logical stage in the process of de-Stalinization. Police terror, which was decisively curbed as a political step without regard to economic considerations, was, however, an essential element in the traditional Stalinist system of a command economy. Terror ensured that the economic directives issued by the ruling elite would be followed to the letter. It allowed no criticism either of the specific decisions taken at a higher rung of economic administration or of the broad outlines of established economic policy. It enabled the central authorities to impose excessive forced savings on all strata of the population. It enabled them to bleed agriculture white for the sake of capital accumulation in industry. It kept the workers quiet in the face of unprecedented exploitation. It provided manpower—forced labor, if necessary—wherever it was needed. Finally, it kept the managerial class in check. When the use of police terror had to be abandoned, the need arose for evolving other methods to keep the economic wheels in motion.

The end of the system of terror has given economists and other social thinkers a chance to speak more freely and to point out great flaws in the traditional system of planning and management. They have even been able to elaborate the outlines of an alternative economic model. The net effect of all this was that the ruling oligarchy and the administrative bureaucracy found themselves in the unenviable position of defending an economic system which was not only vulnerable on theoretical grounds, but which had also failed to produce promised results and had, in fact, led to economic stagnation.[3]

This explains, at least partially, why the ruling oligarchies throughout the Soviet bloc decided to adopt a new economic system, although they knew full well that this was bound to undermine their monopoly of power.

The primary reason for stagnation was a lack of alternative options. By the late 1950s, the command economy had outlived any economic usefulness it ever had. There were diminishing returns from the huge inputs of investment and such outlays "were no longer able to secure the predetermined growth rate, regardless of its social value."[4] Indeed, especially in the more industrialized countries of Eastern Europe, the growth rate began to stagnate.[5] At the same time, statistical evidence began to accumulate disclosing the growing disparity between actual output and effective demand (both in the consumer and the capital sectors). As a result, stocks of unwanted products began to grow at an alarming rate, disturbing the ratio between accumulation and consumption beyond tolerable levels. It was becoming more and more evident that production was losing touch with concrete market requirements, which could no longer be centrally predetermined. This meant (as a prominent Polish economist put it) that "a basic contradiction had developed between the old methods of planning and industrial management—evolved at another stage of economic development—and the current aims of economic policy, as determined by an objective need to substitute intensive for extensive methods of promoting economic growth."[6]

What, in fact, happened was that the command economy had become a victim of its own partial successes. Despite the overriding emphasis on capital goods industries and on growth-oriented investment policies, pursued for more than a decade, by the late 1950s most of the East European economies had attained a sufficient degree of industrialization to emerge from a classic sellers' market noted for acute scarcity of goods in demand into a limited buyers' market. It was at this point that the basic shortcomings of the traditional centralized command economy began to be felt in earnest. The most obvious symptom of inefficiency and wastefulness was the objectively unexplainable phenomenon of "overproduction of unsaleable and unwanted goods in the midst of the still prevailing scarcities."[7] All this proved that the command economy was simply unable to cope with the problems involved in the transition from what was predominantly investment demand, determined by the central planners, to effective consumer demand. In this new situation, the *a priori* determination of economic targets tended to become more and more difficult, since consumer demand is determined by the not easily predictable aggregate requirements, desires, and even caprices of the population—especially if primary needs are being satisfied in full. As the result of all this, the ruling elite began *contre coeur* to realize that the traditional methods of planning and economic management had become unworkable and were hampering further economic growth.

II

Having finally accepted the need for change, the understandable reaction of the ruling elites has been a tendency to contain the indispensable economic reforms within the traditional political and economic system. Although objective economic conditions left them no alternative but to initiate qualitative changes in the methods of planning and management, the ruling oligarchies obviously intended to control both the scope and the momentum of economic reforms to such a degree as to preserve the orthodox political and economic institutions that ensured their monopoly of power. *They did not really want a new economic model, but would have been perfectly satisfied with a more efficient and rational version of the old one.*[8] However, even in the early stages of the implementation of economic reforms—at least in those countries that have adopted a more advanced version of the new economic model (such as Yugoslavia, Hungary, and Czechoslovakia before 1969)—it has become increasingly apparent that not only was there little chance of preserving any meaningful vestiges of the traditional economic *modus operandi*, but that the existing political institutions were also likely to be affected by the process of change.

The political impact of economic reform was perceived, of course, by dogmatic elements in the party leaderships and administrative apparatuses, as well as by a multitude of others profiting financially from the traditional economic system. While the latter were mainly concerned about the danger to their vested interests, the former were primarily anxious about the potential impact of economic reforms on ideology and power politics.

With their vital interests at stake, the hardline dogmatists and imperiled opportunists in all countries of Eastern Europe (and the Soviet Union, too) have formed a common front against the onslaught of pragmatic reformers. At first, they avoided frontal attacks and theoretical debates and concentrated instead on delaying tactics. They preferred to operate behind the scenes, often paying lip-service to the need for change, while in fact they were quietly sabotaging the efforts of the reformers. One way or another, they played (and still do) on the inevitable inhibitions and hesitations of the ruling oligarchies, often succeeding in delaying or diluting the necessary reforms.

These delaying tactics finally convinced the reformers that really qualitative changes in the political system were an indispensable condition for implementing their proposed reforms. In the early stages of formulating these reforms, the pragmatists were mainly preoccupied with the purely operational ways and means and organizational structure of the new economic system. But as soon as the first fragmentary reforms were introduced, it became increasingly evident that they could become fully effective only within a different, more pluralistic and participatory political framework. It is indeed quite remarkable that as early as 1965 a well-known Polish economist, having made a detailed survey of the most economic reform-oriented countries in Eastern Europe, reported a nearly unanimous view that "the traditional bureaucratic style of work" was the main obstacle to the proper implementation of reforms, and that the whole problem could be overcome only by meaningful changes (i.e., greater democratization) in the political system.[9]

This close interdependence between the new economic model and institutional changes in the political field was stressed with particular emphasis in all those countries where really qualitative changes in the existing economic system were about to be introduced.

What most reformers were aiming at was a devolution of some of the political power to "democratic representative bodies and to special-interest organizations,"[10] (e.g., parliament, local government bodies, and trade unions). Just as the trade unions and other special-interest organizations should, in the reformer's view, concentrate on defending the specific interests of definite social groups, so the democratic representative bodies ought to have decisive say in all macro-economic decisions affecting the population as a whole. The advocates of socialist pluralism did not pretend that, if such decisions were made by "democratic representative bodies" (and not by the Party oligarchy as hitherto), there would be less likelihood of error of judgment. They argued simply that such a decentralization of the decision-making process is more consistent with the spirit of democratic socialist pluarlism required by the operational patterns of the new economic model. Moreover, they maintained that only through democratization could the *political* model of a "workers' state" develop in harmony with the new system of managing the national economy.

This is precisely what Dubcek and his close associates wanted to do. What actually took place in Czechoslovakia in the brief interval of relative political freedom before the Soviet tanks rolled in is now a matter of historical record. There is little doubt that the process of political democratization acquired a momentum of its own and, for many complex reasons, went much further than what the Dubcek team had envisaged as a necessary precondition for the successful implementation of the new economic model. No one can say for certain whether the trend of events in Czechoslovakia between January and August 1968 was inevitable, since no absolutely comparable situation has ever existed before. The momentum of any social process is influenced by many diverse factors, some of them unique to a given country, period of time, or political situation. In other words, the actual sequence of events in Czechoslovakia might not manifest itself elsewhere.

Yet one basic point should be stressed here: The fact that as soon as the Dubcek team assumed real political power, it insisted that meaningful changes in the political system were a necessary precondition for the effective operation of the new economic model. This was not done under the spell of political euphoria that overtook Czechoslovakia after the downfall of Novotny. It was a deliberate political decision, the theoretical justification for which had been worked out well in advance by many prominent social scientists.

Needless to say, the spectacular dynamics of the political developments in Czechoslovakia, especially between January and August 1968, were to a great degree exceptional. This unprecedented momentum was due primarily to a very specific political situation, which (if Moscow can help it) is not likely to repeat itself anywhere in Eastern Europe, at least not in the foreseeable future. The Brezhnev doctrine was specifically devised to preclude such a contingency. But the actual dynamics of the democratization process is one thing, and the over-all impact of the new economic model on the established political institutions of the orthodox communist state is quite another. There certainly exists a definite cause-and-effect relationship between the implementation of qualitative economic reforms and gradual changes in the traditional power structure. The ruling elite might, for a time, succeed in putting a brake on those political changes and thus keep them under control, but it cannot prevent them altogether. This is precisely what has been happening in Hungary ever since the process of economic reforms was set in motion. And for all its slowness and ambivalence the movement is definitely tending in the same direction as it did in Czechoslovakia. This is hardly surprising, since there are close parallels between the fundamental principles of the Hungarian and Czechoslovak economic models.

Compared with what happened in Czechoslovakia, the trend toward limiting the party's monopoly of power in Hungary has been far less pronounced and certainly much less spectacular. One reason for this was that in Hungary the ruling elite had quite early seized the initiative in introducing the necessary qualitative changes into the traditional economic system and thus made certain (up to a point) that these changes would be put into effect under direct party control. Faced with the alternatives of the traditional command economy and of one based on "socialist market relations," the Hungarian ruling elite held firmly to the middle ground. Pleading that "it was of utmost importance that the extremes be avoided," it decided upon a judicious mixture of far-reaching economic reforms at the micro-economic level and a gradual democratization of the existing power structure.

But the slow pace of the Hungarian democratization process does not detract from two essential factors. While in Czechoslovakia the program of political reforms was mainly proclaimed by ideological dissenters (both within and without the ruling elite), in Hungary the proposed institutional changes do enjoy the full approval of the established center of political power and at least the tolerance of Moscow.[11] In the terms of communist *Realpolitik*, this is certainly the most crucial factor, since—as the Czechoslovak tragedy has amply demonstrated—no meaningful political changes can be implemented anywhere in Eastern Europe without at least the grudging consent of the Kremlin. And since Moscow has, quite obviously, given the Kadar regime the go-ahead sign, one can be fairly optimistic about the prospects of the (limited) democratization process in Hungary.

The second factor is not less significant. It is by no means a coincidence that the Hungarian drive toward a greater degree of democratization gathered momentum only after the invasion of Czechoslovakia. The basic reason for this was, no doubt, as much political as psychological. The Hungarian leadership realized that the powerful shock produced by the brutal military intervention in Czechoslovakia, as well as the vehement attacks in the Warsaw Pact press against Czechoslovak economic reformers, raised serious and deep-rooted concern among Hungarians about the fate of their own new economic model. The fact that the other four invading powers maintained a heavy propaganda barrage against the concept of a "socialist market economy" in general and against the principles of both the Czechoslovak and the Yugoslav economic reforms in particular, did nothing to alleviate this anxiety, especially since so many aspects of the Hungarian model were quite similar to the Czechoslovak one. The Hungarian ruling elite's response was prompt and unambiguous. High-ranking party leaders such as Istvan Szirmai, Karoly Nemeth, and Jeno Fock publicly reassured the country that the reform would continue. Moreover, both official statements and articles in the press promised that it would even be extended to such socio-political areas as scientific research, local administration, and public participation in the decision-making process through democratization of political institutions. These public statements were generally regarded as a definite refusal to give in to internal and external pressures generated by the invasion of Czechoslovakia and a hopeful omen for the future.

III

Both in theory and in practice, the reformist course in Yugoslavia offers striking contrasts to the paths followed in other countries of Eastern Europe. It is hardly necessary to point out that Belgrade's unique status of independence in the Communist galaxy since 1948, and its early and continuing experimentation with "workers' self-government," dating back to 1950-51, have given it a giant lead in the field of economic and political reform. This chapter will not attempt to review those developments, since its purpose is to measure the comparative impact of the reformist movement as a blocwide phenomenon of recent origin. In assessing the present situation in Yugoslavia, the important fact to be borne in mind is that it is the only communist country in which an apparent majority in the ruling elite has sincerely accepted the difficult conclusion that the successful implementation of economic reform requires a new type of Communist party that guides but does not command. Thus, the dominant elements in the Yugoslav establishment, on one hand, and the liberal intellectuals, on the other, are in essential agreement on the need for a change in the party's role in the new system of socialist democracy. They are vehemently opposed on this issue by a still strong minority composed of genuine conservatives, ex-partisan grass-roots leaders, and worried bureaucrats.

At the same time, the progressive Yugoslav establishment and the more radical intellectuals are still poles apart on the issue of practical institutional reforms necessary to transform the role of the party.

Therefore, a clear distinction must be made between the official concept of a gradual evolution of the party's status within the framework of the system of workers' self-government, and the more extreme views expressed by the intellectual wing of the party and an influential pressure group of university professors.

The official position (spelled out repeatedly) starts from the premise that "the party is not an end in itself," but merely a means subordinated to the basic interest of "the economically emancipated working class." Consequently, "the role of the party, the form of its organizations, and its manner of functioning have not been established once and for all," and may be changed in response to a given "specific historical situation." Such changes, it is held, have been going on ever since the system of workers' self-government was introduced. According to this view, all progressives, and first of all the ruling elite, recognize that "the self-managing community of production workers" represents a higher and more complex phase of socialist construction. It is founded on the "free operation of economic laws" and "a commodity-money market." Its key feature is "direct control by producer associations over surplus value." The point then underscored is that "as a result, the political system has undergone a transformation, and the working class has acquired more direct influence over political power."[1,2] In the view of the ruling elite, this transformation has proceeded at a pace and to a degree compatible with the evolution of the economic system.

The members of the Yugoslav intellectual elite tend to agree with the first part of this analysis. They have the same (if not stronger) critical attitude toward bureaucratic forms of socialism, and by and large accept the view that workers' self-management represents a vast improvement over the old command economy. They do not, however, share the party leadership's apparent self-satisfaction with the pace of political reform. The more outspoken among them flatly refuse to accept the establishment's viewpoint that the political changes already effected, or even those contemplated for the near future, are adequate to the country's needs or wishes. Many openly claim that the decentralization of political power has not gone far enough.

One of the early typical statements of this attitude was made by Professor L. Markovic of Belgrade University in an article published by the main party organ, *Borba*. Markovic argued that "neither the state nor the party . . . can contain within the old framework the (new) socialist forces that have ripened in our society." The main political and social problem in Yugoslavia, he wrote, is that the party "claims to do things it can no longer do." The implication of his argument is that a Communist party is no longer capable of leading a modern industrial society. Not only has the party remained essentially unchanged, but it has failed to purge itself sufficiently of the hard-line dogmatists. Therefore, there is always the danger that the hard-core conservatives within the party "who still think in terms of state socialism" might once more gain the upper hand and "evolve into a new bureaucratic class that would try to move the wheels of history backward." The only way to prevent such a development, according to Markovic, is to limit the party's monopoly of power through concrete institutional reforms.[13]

Other Yugoslav political thinkers have gone even further, openly advocating a two-party or even a multi-party system as a more suitable political framework both for accommodating the conflicting interest groups that have crystallized under the economic reforms and for promoting the sense of public participation required for the successful implementation of those reforms. After all, stated one of them, Professor Stevan Vracar, "if a two-party or multi-party system has not threatened the existence of capitalism, but has rather strengthened it, why should not the same thing happen under socialism?"[14]

In another article on the same subject, Professor Vracar starts from the premise that in many Communist countries government "has been transformed, *de facto* as well as *de jure*, into the supremacy of a single party over the (organs of) state, so that all important party decisions are directly translated into legal acts by the top state organs." To avoid the dictatorship of a single party, he argued, it is necessary to destroy the myth that at the present stage of socialist construction there is no alternative to a one-party system. The only effective remedy, in his view, is a multi-party political structure validated in legal form.[15]

A somewhat less extreme solution was proposed by Pedrag Vranicki, Professor of Philosophy at the University of Zagreb. His argument is that Communist parties ought to democratize their internal *modus operandi* to the extent of allowing minority views to be expressed and openly propagated, even after majority views have been decided upon. This democratic process would lead "to the abolition of the (Communist party's) monopoly over the mass information media and allow different opinions to be freely expressed, so that every socialist idea could be voiced during the whole course of a controversy." Thus, Vranicki underwrote Vracar's thesis that pluralistic socialist democracy requires a legalized and politically active opposition. However, he was definitely hostile to the idea of a multi-party system, which he considered incompatible with the basic concept of workers' self-government.[16]

These views may appear to be rather idealistic notions standing no chance of realization and supported only by a minority of dissenters among the intellectual elite. Yet, while the positions taken by Vracar and Vranicki (as well as by some other university professors) represent the extremes of liberal opinion in Yugoslavia, their ideas on the essential issue of political pluralism have been echoed by the more perceptive members of the ruling establishment. For instance, Mijalko Todorovic, then one of the secretaries of the Yugoslav Central Committee and currently President of the Federal Assembly was quoted by Radio Belgrade as having stated that "solutions of conflicts caused by the existence of different interest groups in society must be sought in a free confrontation of the views representing these conflicting interests." The political leadership, stated Todorovic, was well aware that unless a proper forum was made available for the presentation and satisfaction of these various group interests, Yugoslavia might well be "split" into a "multi-party political society."[17]

It follows that—according to Todorovic—unless the ruling elite makes really meaningful concessions to the powerful interest groups in Yugoslav society, it may face the prospect of a spontaneous process of political pluralization that could seriously undermine, if not destroy, the single-party system. The moot questions are: To what extent do these views represent the thinking of the dominant elements in the present Yugoslav establishment, and how far are these elements prepared to go in order to prevent political pluralization? The recent events, including the purge of the Croation party leadership, indicate that this question remains more actual than ever.

IV

To sum up, there seems to be ample proof that the introduction of genuine, qualitative economic reforms in Communist countries encourages the emergence of pluralistic political tendencies. It is also to some extent true that the degree of progress made toward implementing economic reforms determines the intensity of the search for a suitable pluralistic solution. But it is also true that factors other than economic influence the momentum of political change. In Yugoslavia, the process of evolving a participatory pluralistic system is complicated by the major dilemma of how to adapt or integrate the institutional forms of workers' self-management; among the difficult problems to be resolved, for example, is that of granting the Yugoslav trade unions their proper status as a special-interest group. In Czechoslovakia, on the other hand, the semi-revolutionary situation that mushroomed under Dubcek led to a much quicker tempo of political change than the actual progress of economic reform warranted. While the Soviet occupation has brought about the converse situation of a retreat from political reform, a situation that is likely to persist in the foreseeable future, there is hope that the economic reform program will not be completely laid to rest.

In short, no one can predict with any degree of accuracy either the momentum or the final institutional form of qualitative changes in the political systems of the East European bloc—or, for that matter, the degree or intensity of resistance to such changes. Granted that various strategic considerations entered into the decision to invade Czechoslovakia, the enforced retreat from political liberalization since the occupation offers grim evidence that the conservatively-oriented Communist ruling elites are prepared to go to great lengths to defend both the principle and the practice of party supremacy. But barring a bloc-wide return to Stalinism imposed by force (which, even in the unlikely event that it could be achieved, would create economic havoc), the ruling elites must sooner or later come to realize that they "cannot have their cake and eat it too." *If they want genuine economic progress, they must come to accept some degree of encroachment on their political prerogatives.* However long it takes, it seems fairly certain that the era of each communist party's absolute monopoly of power is coming to an end—at least in those countries which have opted for a qualitatively different economic model or are gradually being impelled toward such a decision by economic exigencies.

If this basic assumption is correct, it is possible to offer—if not predictions—then at least conjectures about the direction of future developments in the bloc. One probable trend will be toward solutions separating the party apparatus from the direct process of government. Such a trend is still in an embryonic stage in Hungary, but it has to be borne in mind that Budapest's *economic* reform program—which in many respects is more comprehensive and far-reaching than the Czechoslovak model—was several years in preparation before qualitative changes in the economic system began to be implemented in January 1968, and their full impact has yet to be felt. In Yugoslavia, the evolution of the political system is already well underway, and some new institutional forms of a participatory pluralistic system are beginning to take shape even in the face of strong resistance.

As far as special-interest groups are concerned, the most interesting developments can be expected within the *trade unions*. Economic reforms everywhere, though particularly in the countries which have adopted advanced economic models, have tended to destroy former patterns of labor relations and to focus anew on the basic conflict of interest between management and the working force. The greatly increased prerogatives of enterprise managers make it imperative, from the workers' point of view, to create an effective institutional counterweight. Barring emulation of the Yugoslav "workers' self-government" system in other Communist countries (which seems unlikely), there must be a basic reassessment of the role and the very *raison d'etre* of the trade unions.

In contrast to the workers, the technocrats—although their vital interests are also at stake—are less likely to lean toward the creation of a specific organization to act on their behalf. The most obvious reason for this is that the technocrats seem well on the way toward a gradual takeover of the Communist party itself. The percentage of technocrats and other white collar workers with similar group interests among the party members is growing rapidly, while the percentage of blue-collar workers is dwindling.[18] Moreover, the technocrats already have a strong economic power base of their own and are able to promote their group interests effectively, both at party forums and in government bodies. The change in social structure of the ruling Communist parties is highly significant. For if the trade unions reach a point where they can validly claim to be the sole—or even the major—representatives of the workers' interests, the traditional ideological image of the Communist party as the vanguard of the proletariat will become even more untenable than it already is.

Besides being challenged by the technocrats, the unions, and the workers, the principle of party supremacy is also likely to be undermined by the enhanced roles of the state's administrative apparatus and special interest groups. Thus, even if the one-party system can survive the impact of economic reforms, the party establishment will hardly be able to retain its monopoly of power. What could well happen is that the party may become a microcosm of the inevitable interplay among special-interest groups. *This would mean that, for all practical purposes, the rudiments of a multi-party system would be created within the party itself, if not outside its organizational structure.* But, as things stand now, the return to a genuine multi-party system seems highly unlikely.

Legalized opposition within the institutional framework of a participatory, pluralistic—if still semi-authoritarian—system is quite another matter. One can well envisage organized opposition in representative state bodies, or a special-interest group such as a trade union fighting a decision of the ruling elite that affects the vital interests of its members. Even within the party this type of organized—if not yet legalized—opposition has already emerged in both Yugoslavia and Czechoslovakia; and while the trend has been aborted in Prague, military occupation is a manifestly limited and self-injurious option for the conservative forces. In the end, the course of development seems bound to be determined internally in each country, according to the degree to which it must meet the demands of the modern technological age. And wherever economic reform is genuine, political pressures will be created. Thus, at least in some of the bloc countries, the time may not be far off when not only the expression of dissent but also the advocacy of basic policy alternatives will become a normal and accepted pattern of political behavior in a pluralistic socialist system.

Notes

1. Unsigned Editorial: "Where are We Going?", *Nepszabadsag*, Sept. 22, 1968, and subsequent official statements.

2. Professor Petr Pithart of Prague University, in an interview broadcast over *Radio Bratislava*, May 22, 1967.

3. The pertinent facts of this stagnation are well documented in the article by Professor W. Brus, "Some General Remarks on the Changes in the System of Planning and Management," *Gospodarka Planowa*, Nov. 1, 1966.

4. E. Loebl, "On Dogmatism in Economic Thinking," *Kulturny zivot*, Sept. 28, 1963.

5. "In the last phase of the 1956-1960 period a number of signs appeared indicating that living off the past could not continue much longer. . . . They were apparent not only in the declining growth rate of national income in all the European socialist countries (with the exception of Rumania) . . . but above all in the less than anticipated effectiveness of investments . . . Nor does it seem accidental that the sharpest decline in the rate of growth took place in the most advanced socialist countries. In Czechoslovakia, the average annual rate of growth in the 1961-1965 period was 1.8 percent, as compared to seven percent in the previous five-year period, while in the GDR the figures were 2.8 percent and 8.1 percent, respectively." Cf. W. Brus, op. cit.

6. J. Pajestka, "Some Factors Affecting the Acceleration of Economic Development in our Country," *Nowe Drogi*, Dec. 12, 1962, pp. 66-67.

7. W. Brus, "On Certain Stipulations of Economic Progress," *Zycie Gospodarcze*, Nov. 11, 1962.

8. J. Fock, "The Economic Reform Was Initiated by the Party and It Must Be Carried out under the Leadership of the Party," *Nepszabadsag*, Dec. 1, 1966.

9. J. Keeler, "Across Five Countries—What Has Not Been Done," *Polityka*, Sept. 25, 1965.

10. I. Bystrina, "The New System and Democracy," *Literarni noviny*, Dec. 1966.

11. In the early post-invasion period, Moscow repeatedly and quite emphatically endorsed the Hungarian version of economic reforms, as well as the proposed institutional changes in that country. See: B. Rodionow, "Gathering Speed," *Izvestiya*, Sept. 16, 1968; M. Tiurin, "Steps of Growth," *Izvestiya*, Nov. 14, 1968; V. Gerasimow, "With the Participation of Millions," *Pravda*, Feb. 13, 1969; and M. Timar, "A Country's Reform and Economic Development," *Pravda*, April 22, 1969.

12. M. Pecujlic, "Class and Political Vanguard under Contemporary Conditions of the Struggle for Socialism," *Review of International Affairs* (Belgrade), Jan. 5, 1968 (English-language edition). Pecujlic is a top spokesman for the regime on ideological matters and a member of the Executive Committee (Politburo) of the League of Yugoslav Communists.

13. L. Markovic, "Etatism, Classes, Politics," *Borba*, Jan. 5, 1968.

14. S. Vracar, "Pluralism in Socialist Democracy," *Pregled*, March 3, 1966.

15. S. Vracar, "Party Monopoly and the Political Power of Social Groups," *Gledista*, August-September 1967.

16. P. Vranicki, "The State and the Party under Socialism," *Knjizevne novine*, Oct. 14, 1967.

17. Todorovic's speech as broadcast by *Radio Belgrade*, Jan. 25, 1968.

18. Thus, according to official Yugoslav data, in 1947, "workers" constituted thirty percent of the party membership, while "white collar" employees constituted 14.9 percent. By 1970, the respective figures were twenty-nine percent for "workers" and 37.0 percent for the "white collar" force (with the military, students and peasants accounting for most of the remainder). Cf. *Socijalizam*, nos. 7-8, July-August 1971.

2

The U.S.S.R.: The Reform that Never Was

Alec Nove

Background to Change

The centralized or "Stalin" model of planning, devised in the USSR, was adopted in other countries of the Soviet sphere during the period in which they all, regardless of size, traditions and resource endowment, copied all things Soviet. However, in all these countries this model is being questioned and, to varying degrees, changed. No longer is there any compulsion to copy the Soviet way of doing things in every detail, and so no two countries are alike in the pace and shape of their reforms. The USSR and Hungary are chosen here as examples because the size and key position of the USSR makes it an essential object of study, and because Hungary has gone furthest (Yugoslavia apart) in the direction indicated by the reforming philosophy. It is also significant that the USSR is among the more "conservative" countries in its approach to change.

It is necessary to begin any discussion of the causes of reform by a brief analysis of the purpose and logic of the "Stalin" system and the changing circumstances within which it was operating in the Soviet Union.

These circumstances can be analyzed as follows:

The origin of the "Stalin" system derives from the concept of the "revolution from above." Central control was maximized not just to please the power-hungry leadership, but to change society. If one is seeking rapid structural changes, then market forms expressing the pattern of demand of the existing society are not merely irrelevant but dangerous. Economists who argue in favor of objective criteria become "objective" allies of those political forces opposed to the great leap forward. This helps explain why so many eminent economists of the 1920s went to prison in the 1930s.

The objective of the "revolution from above" was to create extremely rapidly, a heavy industrial base. It involved making sacrifices, assigning priority to key sectors of industrial materials, fuel, and equipment, neglecting the needs of agriculture and the

19

citizenry in general—and all this by methods reminiscent of a war economy (the parallel is Oskar Lange's). In a war economy, the government imposes its choices and ignores market influences. This is why, say in Britain or Germany during World War II, private car manufacturers were not allowed to compete for available metals; these and other vital materials were allocated administratively, at fixed prices.

It was a time of "extensive" investment, with a large reserve of underemployed peasant labor. New industries were being created. Such problems as training factory labor and building great new industrial complexes seemed much more important than "efficiency" or replacing outmoded machinery. New industrial models could in any case be purchased or copied from abroad. What could not be copied from abroad was development economics. There was *no* development economics until after the last war. And even today there is endless argument about the nature of "development strategies" and their connection with static efficiency criteria.

Times gradually changed after the war. Fundamental structural change was no longer a major objective. There was no more "revolution from above." The Soviet economy had grown much more mature, sophisticated, complex. It was increasingly hard to control it from the center in the old way. The labor situation became tighter; it is true that to this day over 30 percent of the labor force is in agriculture, but it consists mainly of old, female, unskilled workers. In many parts of the USSR there developed a shortage of urban labor. After Stalin's death, the despot's iron priorities were substantially modified. More attention was paid to agriculture, housing, consumer goods and services. Various controls over people were relaxed: amnesties emptied the mass of the forced labor camps, and workers could leave their jobs without permission. All these factors created strains representing a growing contradiction between the economic structure and the forces of production. They became the subject of widespread discussion in the USSR in 1956, if not earlier.

Stalin's death and the end of his terror facilitated the process of change by making discussion of the various problems possible. But of course the problems were already there.

The various factors making for reform require some more detailed examination. One factor was and is the *growing complexity* of the Soviet economy. This meant in practice that decisive action was often not taken for lack of time and information. It is a characteristic of the traditional Soviet system of planning that "the plan" is the sole criterion for decision-making. The authorities, in their efforts to transform society, allocate resources without regard to automatically functioning economic forces. Prices, the "law of value," play no allocative role, at least not in the process of deciding *what* to produce. The planning organs have the duty of collecting information about needs—from enterprises about producers' goods, from state retail stores about consumers' goods. This information is combined with instructions from the highest political organs concerning investment policies, growth targets, priorities. In the end, the planners must "translate" all this into *plan-instructions* covering every enterprise's output, delivery, inputs, labor, cost, finance, investment and other plans. The fulfillment of these plans becomes the highest duty of all intermediate and lower echelons of the system.

But the scale of the necessary decision-making process was far too large. There were several consequences:

a. Detailed and balanced plans could be made only for key priority sectors. Other sectors had to make do with what resources were left.

b. The "Center" had to be divided—for purposes of administering and planning the economy—into ministries and departments, each of which developed strong interests of its own. This in practice meant a sort of "polycentric centralism," or "pluralistic monolithism." With the "Center" thus weakened, the various ministries and departments are now *competitors* for resources, especially investment resources.

c. Various plans reached enterprises from different units of the planning hierarchy. Thus, supply and production, finance and investment, labor and costs, were planned by different offices. This created inconsistencies that, along with others, necessitated frequent changes of the plan.

d. Plans had to be aggregated to be manageable. Ton-kilometers, square meters, and millions of roubles, represented quantifications of dissimilar goods, and the product-mix was distorted by the attempt to fulfill plans so expressed. These aggregate totals were *not* arrived at by adding together the elements of which they were composed, but rather by adding a percentage to past plans or past performance, this being the so-called ratchet principle, or planning *"po dostignotomu urovnyu,"* as the Russians say. Hence the familiar distortions: making goods heavy to fulfill plans in tons, choosing more costly variants to fulfill them in roubles, poorer quality to fulfill cost reduction plans, and so on.

e. This contradicted the desire of the authorities to achieve a closer relationship between consumer demand and production. Stocks of unsold goods increased, queues for goods in short supply did not decrease.

f. The inconsistencies of plans, and especially between the supply plan and the production plan (and also frequent changes in plans during the year), encouraged hoarding of materials and under-statements of production potential. These actions led to unnecessary losses and distorted the flow of information upon which plans are based.

g. There was a lack of any built-in incentive to innovate. Grossman once spoke of "routine, inertia, and pressure." The traditional system gave no reward for risk-taking, gave good bonuses to those who went on doing whatever they did before, only more so. Pressure, orders from above, did lead to technical progress in many sectors, yet lack of incentives for change resulted in losses. The lack of direct influence of user-enterprises on their suppliers in the matter of product-mix, already mentioned, also impeded technical progress. In many instances modern and productive equipment was not supplied, because aggregate plans for machinery are more easily fulfilled by making obsolete machines.

All these factors were part of the background to the reforms. They are long-term in the sense that they provide no explanation as to the *date* of any actual reform measure. They raised questions and difficulties with which Stalin's successors somehow had to grapple. The evolution of the economy and of society put these matters on the agenda. But this did not necessarily mean that anything was actually done about them. There were, as we shall see, obstacles to change: inertia, vested interest, habit ideology (or is "ideology" a form in which inertia and vested interest are expressed?). After all, the existence of inefficiency is not in itself proof of ineffectiveness. The Western war economies were in many respects inefficient, but they were tolerated, their inefficiency being a *necessary* cost of concentrating resources for war. In the case of Russia, we must also mention *national-historical* tradition, a factor which distinguishes the country from most others and which deserves a paragraph to itself.

The role of the state in Russian economic development, and in Russian society, has been noted by many historians. Whatever merit state intervention may have had, it contributed to the relative weakness of spontaneous social-economic forces. To keep up with the more developed West, or to catch up when the gap became too great for safety, Russian monarchs organized society to serve the state, and serfdom as an institution arose as part of this process, as a means of supporting the Tsar's civil and military servants. Stalin was, at least in this sense, the successor of the modernizing Tsars, and his actions found some response in the historical subconscious of many of the people. This tradition in Russia, absent in other countries, helps to explain the contrast between the attitudes and policies of the Soviet Union and those of its European allies.

All this does not answer the questions: Why were the reforms adopted when they were? Why were they so widely debated? Perhaps the following reasons are among the most important:

a. Stalin's death and the abandonment of mass terror led to the expression of criticism that had previously been suppressed, and this had a gradual effect on official thinking.
b. The attempt by Stalin's successors to satisfy many wants simultaneously led to economic overstrain and contributed not only to dangerous disequilibria but also to a sharp *decline in growth rates*, especially after 1958. This made the authorities particularly receptive to new ideas.
c. The failure of the *sovnarkhoz* (regionalization) experiment of 1957-64, the agricultural troubles of the last Khrushchev years and the administrative confusions which accompanied them led to a widespread realization that something new was needed. The "something new" evidently had to provide greater managerial autonomy, based on criteria other than those of fulfilling plans issued from above.
d. The experience and experiments in other eastern European countries were having some influence in Russia.
e. The rapid development of computer and mathematical techniques, the attractive possibilities of their use in planning, presented new problems and opportunities. Such influential senior scholars as the late Academician Nemchinov played a significant part in convincing the leadership that something ought to be done.

The reforms in all the countries of Eastern Europe were, in varying ways, seeking a new balance between central planning and a decentralized market (or "commodity-money") mechanism. No one really imagined that basic investment decisions affecting the whole shape and proportions of the economy could be left to the market in a country where the state owns the instruments of production and where there is no stock exchange and thus only a limited kind of capital market. No one really doubted that the product-mix—e.g., of cloth, farm implements, hats, dyestuffs or shoes—should accord with the requirements of the users. Since consumer demand could not be determined by the central planners, there would have to be more direct links between customer and supplier. Prices would therefore have to act as information carriers, and profit would then have to act as an important part of managerial incentives to make it worth while to satisfy demand.

Note that the proposed changes would not introduce incentives where previously there were none: the "Stalin" model included substantial bonus payments to managers, but they were paid for plan fulfillment, i.e., for obeying orders from above. They provided no inducement for the managers to take decisions of their own. All the reformers were agreed as to the necessity of a closer link between prices, profits, and resource allocation, i.e., the introduction of some elements of a "socialist market." But opinion differed widely as to the proper balance between market and plan.

To make reforms a reality, it would plainly be necessary to dismantle all or most of the current production and supply planning procedures. These go together. Obviously, so long as the allocation of inputs by administrative supply organs continued, each productive unit would have to be told what to produce, since one firm's input is another firm's output. The supply planning system involves designating customers and suppliers, and so eliminates competition. Real reform requires the elimination of supply planning.

Some Soviet-Hungarian Contrasts

Not long ago the literary journal *Novyi mir*[1] published an account of a visit to Hungary by a Soviet citizen named P. Volin. His reaction, as he wishes to convey it, was one of naive surprise. You mean to say that in Hungary managers are *not* told what to produce? They are allowed to make and sell what the customers wish? They are free to choose their own suppliers? They can buy what they like, even foreign-made commodities? Do Ministries *really* not interfere? Suppose the wrong goods are made? Volin asks his Hungarian host literally. "Suppose the enterprise decides to make not what is needed, but what is simpler and easier to make? Suppose, to take a very simple example . . . a factory decides to stop making cups and increases the output of plates, although the state needs cups. Can it simply issue instructions (on its own authority)?"

The Hungarian replies: "The state actually needs neither cups nor plates. The *people* need them. People buy them in shops. The shops can buy plates or cups from several enterprises. They can also import them from abroad. Therefore the people will not be left without cups." There must be competition, of course. Some will then win, others lose: "The market must be a real market and not a spurious one. Otherwise we will have to return to administrative methods of control. And a real market requires competition."

The tone of Volin's article suggests that he had great sympathy with what the Hungarians were doing, that he wished that things had also changed similarly in the USSR.

However, change in the USSR is slow. The essential fact is that no real *change of model* is yet contemplated, or, if it has been contemplated, the authorities have changed their minds. There has been a reform, it is true, but of the old system and within the old system. Let us illustrate this proposition with a series of quotations.

Hungary[2]

Enterprises should be free to decide "what and how much they want to produce and market... from what enterprises and in what quantities they purchase inputs."

Prices "should balance supply and demand.... The value judgments of the market should express themselves in prices.... Competition between enterprises... will stimulate efficiency. There should be an active role... for the market."

USSR

"Right-wing opportunists... argue for 'market socialism' and for competition between enterprises. This has nothing to do with Leninist principles of socialist management... Some argue... that the customer should find his own supplier, and the supplier his own customer. This must be rejected, as it implies an absolutizing of the laws of the market and of supply and demand, the development of competition between suppliers, and an underestimation of the role of the center. It is wrong to abandon the practice of (planning by) compulsory quantitative indicators."[3]

"Market prices are, in our view, alien to our economy and contradict the task of centralized planning. It is... incorrect to imagine that prices should balance supply and demand. The balance between demand and supply... is the concern of the planning organs."[4]

"Freedom to choose between domestic and imported goods . . . and to decide whether to seal goods in domestic or foreign markets . . . should exist."

"It is impossible to agree to proposals to permit enterprises and associations to operate on international markets other than through the Ministry of Foreign Trade."[5]

Thus the Soviet official view is hostile to the underlying concepts of market socialism and is not prepared to recognize the logic of "active," information-carrying, prices. Much necessarily follows from this, as we shall see.

Soviet Controversies and the New Official Ideology

Many Soviet reformers advocated something very different from the above official position. A whole essay could readily be devoted to the many schools which contended, and to some extent still contend. Some go as far as to cause other, even quite radical reformers to label them as "free market dogmatists" (the words are A. Birman's).[6] Birman himself would like to see the abolition of most or all of the system of material allocation and the basing of most enterprise plans on contracts with customers, relying on the market. Liberman achieved world-wide fame by emphasizing the key role of profits with the slogan: "What is good for society must be profitable for the enterprise," in the pages of *Pravda*. The virtues of supply-and-demand-balancing prices, the logic of socialist market relations, their conformity with a properly-understood Marxian economic theory, were extolled by Novozhilov in Leningrad and Petrakov in Moscow, who have also been advocating the widespread use of mathematics, of programming techniques. Kantorovich urged the adoption of the so called "O.O.O.'s," the Russian initial letters for "objectively determined valuations," i.e., the use of prices derived from a mathematical plan-program.[7]

The director of the Central Economic-Mathematical Institute (TsEMI), Fedorenko, wrote and spoke extensively about the "theory of optimal planning." He rejected accusations of "bourgeois marginalism." True, his theory uses marginal concepts. However, the fact that such concepts are misused by "bourgeois apologists" is no ground for "accusing of 'marginalism' those experts who work out

the means of achieving optimal results in a socialist society."
Fedorenko then outlined a methodology as follows: "The central
planning organ, guided by the experience gained in constructing an
objective consumption function for society, and some other preliminary considerations, values the utility of various goods and the
possibility of reproducing them in relation to the availability of
productive resources at that given moment. It hands down these
valuations to lower production units (sectors, enterprises). These,
having obtained guideline prices for resources and for their output,
draft a local plan for developing production. In doing so they
endeavor to maximize the local criterion, for instance profits. Having
drafted its own plan variant (on the basis of prices handed down
from above and the local optimality criterion), each production unit
sends it back to the central planning organ." Then—according to
Fedorenko—the center aggregates these plans, discovers some surpluses and deficits in relation to availability and needs, and hands
down a different set of prices. On this new basis the 'locals' draft
another plan. By this iterative method, which computers make
possible, one can arrive at a balanced plan with rational prices, and
then the search for profits will stimulate an approach to the
optimum. But this cannot possibly cover all the millions of items of
which a fully disaggregated plan is composed. So the detailed
product-mix will be a matter for enterprises to decide along with
their customers. Detailed prices would also often be decided without
central control, "in the process of this special kind of 'socialist
competition'." The behavior of consumers in the market would be a
vital source of information about demand: "In this way the commodity-money mechanism plays in a socialist society the role of a
regulator, with feedback effects not only in the sphere of production
but also of consumption." Further, "since these prices balance
supply and demand, they play the economic function of a 'market'
or commodity-money mechanism. . . . Concretely this means that
prices are based on *social utility*. . . . The marginal social utility of
any commodity (production resource) is inversely related to the
quantity available."[8]

It is worth noting that a multi-level iterative planning process has
been much discussed in Hungary, especially in the work of J. Kornai
and T. Liptak.

Fedorenko was looking forward to a synthesis between plan and
market, with consumers, management and planners alike responding
to prices at which supply and demand balance. He envisaged a
micro-economic market. He would doubtless have agreed with
another reformer, who asserted that without a market *valuation*

planners would not know whether their plans were correct.[9] The "objective function" is based on demand. Indeed, what other objective function can there be? To assert that the party leaders' preferences could serve as the criterion of optimality is open to one devastating objection: How are even the party leaders themselves to know that they are right? They too need a criterion. They may prefer a high growth rate, or modern weapons, or reduced consumption of vodka. But a disaggregated plan for production and investment consists mainly of items which the leadership cannot logically "prefer." Either one is concerned with consumer satisfaction, or with the best means to achieve given ends (e.g., plastics versus metals, or machine X versus machine Y). By this I do not mean that non-economic preferences are irrational. Obviously regional or strategic policy considerations enter into decision-making. However, it remains necessary to distinguish and identify the nearest practicable approximation to an *economic* optimum, and this cannot usefully be so defined as to open the door wide to political arbitrariness. Even the politicians will not thank their economic advisers for depriving them of a criterion for decision-making, which is the consequence of basing plans on the preferences of politicians!

Some Western critics imagined that the mathematical school would be "centralizers." This is not necessarily the case, and for at least one good reason: A fully disaggregated central plan would have to include literally millions of separately identifiable commodities, produced by hundreds of thousands of enterprises of all sizes, involving millions of production-and-supply links, and requiring a quite impracticable volume of information. Furthermore, most of this information—e.g., on the detailed product-mix—arises from market relations. So the bulk of Soviet mathematical economists support the "socialist market" solution.

There have always been people who opposed this whole approach, as they also opposed Liberman's proposals and Kantorovich's theories. However, the opposition has seemed much stronger of late, possibly because "market socialism" has been associated with the Czech heresy of Ota Sik, and the bulk of official opinion seems to have hardened in a conservative mould. We shall see that this attitude has halted the reform process, with relatively little having been accomplished.

Here are some examples of the currently dominant counter-arguments:

"This concept of 'market socialism' occupies a special place amid various anti-Marxist theories of socialism. It is adopted by right-wing revisionists as an integral part of the general conception of 'democratic' or 'human' socialism, and is also used in the imperialists' "policy of 'building bridges' and 'quite counter-revolution.' " Furthermore, "the functioning of the market mechanism creates wide disparities in income between enterprises and sectors and between different categories of working people." Finally, "as may be seen, contrary to the conceptions of many bourgeois economists, the central questions of economic reform are not concerned with weakening but with strengthening the centralized basis of planning. . . ."[10]

There is also an attack on the mathematicians: "The bridge between mathematics and economics has not been built, and indeed the interrelationship between the two disciplines has not been defined."[11] Significantly, the well-known statistician, A. Boyarski, joins in the offensive. Of course, he adovcates the use of mathematical methods. However, he attacks Fedorenko's whole construct for being based on subjective marginal utility theory. Prices cease to reflect "value," and marginal social utility is substituted in their place. Boyarski cites Marx's opposition to the view that different goods ("meat, wool, wine") have the common property of utility; no, their only common property is that they are the products of labor. In any case, says Boyarski, the Fedorenko model cannot be applied in real life and amounts only to promises for the future. A simple numerical example is used by Boyarski to criticize the proposition that marginal pricing—or "objectively determined valuations"—would lead to optimal utilization of scarce materials such as oil and gas, and his conclusion is: "The question of who is to continue to use oil and who is to change over to gas is best decided by the planning center."[12]

The economist A. Vikentyev takes a similar line, but on a non-mathematical level. He accuses various writers of wrongly understanding the economic reform adopted in 1965 as the replacement of administrative by economic methods: "Of course this is not the essence of the (party) decisions. . . . The reform does not reject administrative methods which, based on the utilization of the economic laws of socialism, are the necessary condition of the development of the national economy."[13] The author attacks the identification of centralization with arbitrariness. If the center's plan-instructions are correct, then they are "economic" and not arbitrary. Indeed, he goes so far as to say that: "Soviet planning and administration, taken as a whole, have successfully fulfilled their tasks, principally because they have rested on a sound scientific base. Therefore planning taken as a whole *has always been optimal*."[14] Vikentyev even rejects the critique of centralized methods made by

Kronrod, himself a moderate who has criticised Kantorovich and other reformers.

Vikentyev has a long record of dogmatic conformism behind him, and his ideas are not worth a minute's time, save in one respect: A few years ago his worthless dogmatism would not have been published. Yet in the meantime it has become a legitimate, although extreme statement of the position of the counter-reformers. His general position is consistent with Sitnin's and the previous quotations from *Pravda*, as well as with another *Pravda* attack by the influential I. Kuzminov on "new models of socialism."[15] The reformers, whether mathematical economists or not, have been repulsed. True, the computer and mathematics are being used and will continue to be used in the process of planning. True also, changes have been made in various aspects of the "traditional" system, and these will be described below. However, the old system, whether of ideas or of organizational-economic substance, has survived any fundamental change.

The Reform That Never Was

The September 1965 reforms appeared, on the surface, to inaugurate a period of fundamental changes. Certainly this was the opinion of a number of Soviet economists at the time. "All our reforms have so far consisted in changing labels on the doors of the same officials; now it is going to be different," declared one economist. He was wrong.

Yet apparently there were some noteworthy changes. Let us recapitulate them:

a. The abolition of the regional *sovnarkhozy*, the restoration of economic ministries, the reconcentration of planning functions in *Gosplan*, with material supplies organized by *Gossnab* (the State Committee on Supplies).

b. The reduction of the number of compulsory indicators planned from above. However, the following are still so planned:
   1. Value of sales *(realizatsiya)*
   2. "The basic nomenclature of output"
   3. The wages-fund total
   4. Profits in roubles
   5. Profitability as a percentage of capital
   6. Payments to and out of the state budget
   7. Centralized investments and new capacity

8. "Basic tasks in the introduction of new technique"
9. Material supply.

Among the many abandoned indicators are the value of gross output and the cost reduction plan.

c. The computation of profits as a percentage of capital was accompanied by the (gradual) introduction of a capital charge, a percentage of an enterprise's capital payable annually into the state budget. New price lists, based on cost *plus* a percentage levied on capital, went into operation in July 1967; these greatly diminished the number of unprofitable enterprises.

d. A larger proportion of investments would henceforth be financed by returnable interest-bearing credits.

e. It was intended gradually to expand wholesale trade in producers' goods, thereby partly replacing their administrative allocation.

f. There was a total recasting of managerial incentives, which now were to be paid out of profits. There are three funds financing, respectively, personal material incentives (for labor and management), amenities, and decentralized investments. The computation of the three incentive funds was and is still exceedingly complex. They are a function of the following elements:

1. Planned profits, profit rate *(rentabel'nost')*, and sales *(realizatsiya)*, usually a combination of *two* of these.
2. The size of the wage fund, or, in the case of payments into the investment fund, the value of capital.
3. The "norm" applicable to the given enterprise or sector. (Thus in one case a 1 percent planned increase in profits might result in a payment of 0.3 percent of the wage fund into the material incentives fund, while in another case, the figure could be 0.2 percent or 0.5 percent, and so on).
4. All the above calculations are modified if the enterprise's results are above or below the plan. (Achievements in excess of plan are subject to a reduced "norm" of payment into the incentive funds, so as to discourage concealment of productive potential.)
5. There are preconditions: The enterprise must fulfill all or most of the compulsory plan indicators listed above and, since 1968, must also ensure that its total payments to labor (including any bonuses out of profits) do not exceed the rise in labor productivity.

In the Shchekinsk chemical combine, a new idea is being tried out: that of letting the employees share the economies in wages due to a reduction in the labor force. (This is exceptional so far.)

The incentive schemes are barely comprehensible and often contradictory. Thus, to take but one example, an economy in wages could have the effect of *reducing* the incentive fund, since this is computed not as a percentage of the (increased) profits but of the *reduced* wage fund. The sales indicator, which is in roubles and in gross terms (in the sense of including the value of purchased inputs) is frequently inconsistent with the profits indicator. Since the main object is to fulfill planned increases in sales and profits, it has become "rational" to avoid too rapid an increase and keep some cash on hand for subsequent years. In any case, as more and more enterprises were transferred to the "new system," old ministerial habits reasserted themselves. Plans are altered arbitrarily, even retroactively, by the ministry; instructions are issued on matters which are supposed to be within the competence of enterprise management, and so on. Protests have frequently appeared in the press about the arbitrary disruption of long-established supply links by ministries striving for "ministerial self-sufficiency" or seeking to ensure priority in supplies for "their" enterprises, thereby duplicating or contradicting the supply network of *Gossnab*.[16]

These deficiencies or contradictions must be seen as the *consequences of non-reform*. Prices do not reflect demand or scarcities save by coincidence. The price recomputations of 1967 were still based on cost-plus, though it is now cost *plus* an amount which includes a rate of return on capital. The capital charge cannot in practice have much effect on demand for capital from below, insofar as it is included in the offical prices. In the same way, higher prices for inputs have little effect on demand for them, or have even at times the effect opposite to that intended, so long as the higher-priced inputs are included in costings and in the official price. (The resultant increase in total value of output and sales "improves" plan performance in roubles.) Such prices as these are useless as indicators of economic behavior. They do not transmit information. Nor are they really intended to do so. The power to allocate resources and to take production decisions remains with the central authorities; it is exercised by the revived industrial ministries, *Gosplan*, and *Gossnab*, under the general supervision of the higher party organs. Chronic excess demand, particularly for investment goods, provides the rationale for administrative allocation based on priorities. Indeed, with existing prices the profit motive cannot operate rationally. There is no connection between profit and need, only between profit and (planned) cost. It is interesting to note that current doctrine regards an increase in profits due to a change in the product-mix or in inputs as somehow "illegitimate." Profits should be "cleansed" *(ochishcheny)* of such elements before being considered as indicators of efficiency.[17] Yet this implies that both the product-mix and the inputs of the enterprise are laid down in a plan initiated or approved at ministerial or departmental *(glavk)* level. It logically follows that the supply plans, made in one or another of the central bodies, cover the major part of industrial output, and that both output and its delivery to designated customers must form part of obligatory plan-orders from above. This is the essence of the old system. It survives today.[18]

The system has an inner logic which defies gradual change.

The elimination of some item from central production, allocation, or investment plans usually has two consequences: The necessary inputs cease to be available, because they are fully committed to *planned* outputs or investments; and the desired goods may not be produced at all, since no effective market-links exist to replace the "traditional" obligatory plan-order.

The "traditional" system, let it be re-emphasized, was based on central administrative assessment of need, upon which basis instructions were issued and plans formulated. In Hungary a new basis has been found, while in the USSR the older pattern remains with little change.

Experiments continue in an effort to improve the system. Indeed, it may be cogently argued that it works better on the "ministerial" basis than it did under the *sovnarkhozy*. There is, after all, no acute crisis; output continues to rise, and living standards are slowly improving.

The present conservative-minded leadership reacts adversely to radical ideas in any field. It is currently attracted to the idea of basing industrial administration on intermediate bodies, the *industrial associations* or trusts *(ob'edineniya)*. These have spread in many industries and are amalgamations of enterprises in the same sector and/or area, under the general authority of an economic ministry. Sometimes the constituent enterprises have been virtually eliminated as autonomous bodies, being relegated to a status similar to that of the workshop *(tsekh)* within an enterprise. Sometimes they retain their separate identity. There are experiments in turning ministerial *glavki* into a species of industrial association, and indeed of putting them and whole ministries on commercial cost-accounting.

Some Western critics regard the move towards industrial associations as "anti-liberal," as yet another move to restrict managerial autonomy and market relations. This appears to me to be only partly true. The Soviet industrial enterprise is usually one factory. Western experience suggests that in many sectors the large corporation, which includes many factories, is the most efficient managerial unit. Insofar as the Soviet rulers are seeking a Soviet equivalent of DuPont, General Electric and Krupp, they can hardly be criticized for conservative resistance to necessary change. However, the industrial association is also doubtless seen by the "conservatives" as an alternative to markets, competition, and similar new-fangled notions.

The point concerning the corporation is only one of many which some of the more naive would-be reformers are inclined to overlook. Perhaps they visualize a market model of the textbook kind and compare the Soviet economy with it. Yet the problems of economies of scale and of externalities cannot be handled within the confines of a model in which they are assumed not to exist. This criticism can be directed equally at the constructs of Fedorenko and of Liberman. Though the former is much more sophisticated than the latter, both envisage a system within which the profitability of the parts adds up to—or is in conformity with—the profitability of the entire economy. Yet this has never been achieved within the confines of the Western corporation: Its very existence is due in large part to the "internalization of externalities," to the fact that profitability is more clearly appreciated at the headquarters of DuPont than in each of the units composing the corporation. Nor can one assert that only political resistance stands in the way of adopting the mathematicians' advice. Some critics of the various mathematical models have a sound basis for their caution as to the applicability of these models to real life. We have only to look at some of the best-known Western growth models. At best, they explain or forecast the behavior of semi-autonomous economic forces. They are not and cannot be a substitute for either operational administrative centralization or for devolution of micro-economic decision-making to management acting within a market.

There are other unsolved questions: The link between incentives based on profits and a non-existent capital market; the emergence of uncontrolled and perhaps undeserved income inequalities; the possible danger of unemployment; the cost of competition (and it has a cost); the problem of bankruptcy, and so on.

Nonetheless, despite very real objective difficulties, it must surely be accepted that *the major obstacle to change lies in a combination of inertia, habit and self-interest*. The party and state bureaucracies are accustomed to work in "traditional" ways, to interfere directly so as to enforce priorities. Not least of these, to this day, are military priorities connected with the cost of the arms and space race. To this some would add ideology, the Marxist-Leninist stress on deliberate planning as against the "anarchic" market. Others argue that the opponents of reform clothe their practical objections in ideological garb, selecting their quotations from Lenin from the period up to 1920, while such reformers as Lisichkin cite the Lenin of NEP in support of his "market" ideas. Whether due to interest, habit or ideology, or all three, the fact remains that opposition is strong among members of the political machine, and the Czechoslovak events of 1968 have strengthened the hand of the conservatives, as we have seen. One of the principal contrasts with the Hungarian experience is that in Hungary the "traditional" system had only been in operation for a few years, whereas few in the USSR can remember living under any other than a centrally planned economy. To these factors must be added the much greater dependence of Hungary upon foreign trade and her much lesser concern with arms and space expenditures. Also, the Hungarian communist leadership is far less determined upon, or confident in its rights to impose, tight party control over the operations of the country's economy.

Conclusion

1723169

When I was in the Soviet Union in 1967 and remarked upon the slow progress in implementing even the modest reform measures of 1965, I was told by my Soviet colleagues: "Change must be gradual, but we are on the way. Come back in two years, and you will hardly recognize the system." I came back in 1969, and it was all very familiar. These same economists were much more cautious in forecasting the adoption of major reform measures. The more radical opinions seldom find their way into the press; the "conservatives" seem to be in control. The contrast with Hungary is striking. It is interesting to note that the Hungarian "new model" is tolerated, even cautiously described in the Soviet press—as in the articles by Friss and by Volin—and much discussed privately by academic staff and students, as I heard for myself in Moscow University. Yet the Czechoslovak proposals of 1968, the ideas of Ota Sik, are denounced as heretical. The explanations of this apparent contradiction are surely political: The Hungarian leadership, in full control of the organs of mass communication, has been careful not to claim the discovery of a "new model," has played on muted strings. There has been no association in Hungary between economic reform and political liberalization, no doctrine of "socialism with a human face"—a doctrine which implies the existence of socialism with an inhuman face.

The question arises: What next in the USSR? The more progressive and original minds in the Soviet economics profession have been arguing for years that the "traditional" system is inefficient, that it has outlived its usefulness, that it stands in the way of the effective utilization and rational expansion of productive forces. It continues to serve as a means of enforcing priorities. It operates adequately in some sectors of heavy industry that are relatively easy to plan in the old way (steel, electricity, coal, cement, and similar relatively homogeneous commodities). The familiar chronic diseases are still causing trouble: Over-taut planning, lack of balance between production and supply plans, between the investment plan and the output of building materials and equipment, resistance to innovation and to technical progress at the lower echelons, distortion of local initiative by the need to simulate plan fulfillment, and so on. The need for change is urgent, even though, as already pointed out, there is no immediate crisis, no demoralization or stagnation such as provided the powerful impetus to new ideas in Czechoslovakia in 1962 and afterwards.

Crystal-gazing is an imperfect science. Conservatism is strong, and not only in Russia! The adaptation of all established structures to change is a painful and slow business. Even to change the organization and methods of a university is no simple job, as all of us must readily agree from our own experience. Resistance to change is very strong in the political organs of the USSR, but it could be overcome, in my view, by a combination of two circumstances. First, by a clear realization that the present economic system is responsible for continued relative backwardness in the competition with the West; at present, Soviet leaders seem to think that the system's admitted inadequacies can be corrected by minor procedural and organization changes. Second, a firm leader or group of leaders must now only be committed to reform, but have the power and will to prevail over the party and state machine. No such leader or leaders seem to exist today, and certainly Brezhnev has neither the power nor the will to do the job.

Change towards greater reliance on market elements will come. The old way has been outgrown. But in the immediate future there is no sign of any major changes in either theory or practice. Many of us have underestimated the conservatism of the "establishment" and the strength of inertia. Some hold that any major reform requires changes in the political structure, affecting particularly the power of the Communist party. Others point out that one could conceive of a greater reliance on managerial autonomy and rational calculation without there being any move towards a relaxation of political controls. There is no time or space to pursue this argument raised by

Gamarnikov here; it is only one of several questions which cloud our vision of the future.

Notes

1. No. 3, 1969, pp. 159-164.
2. *Resolution of the Hungarian Workers' Party* (undated, probably 1967).
3. *Pravda*, Sept. 26, 1969.
4. Sitnin (Chairman of Price Committee, Gosplan), *Ekonomicheskaya gazeta*, no. 25, 1967, pp. 10 ff.
5. *Ekonomicheskaya gazeta*, no. 21, 1968.
6. *Novyi mir*, no. 1, 1967, p. 174.
7. All this is described at length in my *The Soviet Economy* (3rd edition, 1969, pp. 261-271, 311-320).
8. Cited from N.P. Fedorenko: *O razrabotke sistemy optimalinovo funktsioniravaniya ekonomiki* (Moscow, 1968), pp. 34-38.
9. G. Lisichkin argues along these lines in *Plan i rynok* (Moscow, 1966).
10. Yu. Ol'sevich, *Voprosy ekonomiki*, no. 4, 1969, pp. 97, 101.
11. Ya. Gerchuk, in ibid., p. 109.
12. *Voprosy ekonomiki*, no. 8, 1969, p. 115.
13. Ibid., p. 129.
14. Ibid., p. 131. Emphasis his.
15. *Pravda*, April 16, 1969.
16. A few recent examples of such complaints are *Sotsialisticheskaya industriya*, Aug. 9, 1969, p. 2, or A. Shternov, deputy chairman of Gosplan of the Ukraine, *Ekonomicheskaya gazeta*, no. 30, 1969, p. 8.
17. This doctrine was enunciated at Moscow University in April 1969. When the lecturer (Osad'ko) spoke of "cleansing" profits of extraneous elements, one student whispered: "He means removing Ota Sik from profits."
18. This finding does not need to be altered in the light of subsequent events, including the 24th Party Congress of 1971; if at all, a reintroduction of mandatory features has become noticeable.

3

Bulgaria: Tempest in a Teapot

L. A. D. Dellin

Introductory Remarks

Bulgaria, too—like practically all the other Communist states of Eastern Europe—has been embarked on the path of economic reform during the 1960s.[1] Indeed, when the Bulgarian reform blueprint was first spelled out officially at the end of 1965, after a protracted period of preliminary discussion and experimentation, it was optimistically viewed by some Western analysts as heralding a more substantial move away from the Soviet model of a centralized, command economy—at least in certain key respects (notably, planning decentralization and pricing reform)—than was envisaged in the reform plans of some other East European Communist regimes. Actually, as further systematized and elaborated in 1966 and 1967, the blueprint turned out to be less "advanced" than it had appeared to be at first, but its direction was nevertheless still forward—that is, away from Stalinist-type centralized planning and controls.

In 1968, however, there was a clear-cut reversal of direction. While still referring to the "new system of management" evolved in the preceding years, the regime in fact altered the pre-1968 blueprint so drastically as to virtually replace it with a new one strengthening some of the very features which the regime had earlier set out to downgrade. In a very real sense, therefore, it is appropriate to survey the zigzag course of Bulgarian economic reform in terms of two distinct blueprints rather than just one, with 1968 marking the dividing line between them.

It is true that, looking in retrospect, the 1968 reversal toward centralization tends to support those who questioned the extent and even the need of economic reform in Bulgaria. Yet the argument of inverse correlation between level of development and command (lesser development—greater command) appears to be too deterministic in theory and too restrictive in practice even within the Communist-State framework (viz. Yugoslavia) to be fully plausible. Moreover, the Bulgarian economy in the early 1960s, despite its high

39

growth rates and rapid industrialization (and partly because of them) had its share of problems comparable although not necessarily identical to those experienced by almost all other command economies of the Soviet Bloc, which in itself counselled reforms. Last, but not least, the dramatic structural changes in the economy and the paucity of domestic resources to support them forced an even greater reliance on imports, which required a greater efficiency of domestic production—to meet competition—in the export field.[2]

Thus, there were many good reasons for reforms, although by no means as pressing as, for example, in Czechoslovakia. However, it is ironic that the quest for economic reforms was officially announced (and perhaps decided upon) only after the appearance of the noted Liberman article of September 1962 and Khrushchev's sympathetic reaction to it, thus providing new evidence of the too obvious and consistent toeing of the "Soviet line" by the Bulgarian leadership. In subsequent years, as well, Soviet developments remained a guide to Bulgarian reform trends: The "Theses" appeared a few months after the Soviet industrial reform of September 1965 and the 1968 reversal followed the Soviet preference for mathematical solutions of economic problems within the framework of substantially centralized planning and management.

In the following pages, the salient features of the pre-1968 blueprint will first be analyzed principally on the basis of the three major official documents which shaped it: (1) the "Draft Theses" of December 1965,[3] in which the proposed reforms were first outlined in systematic fashion; (2) the decisions of the April 1966 Plenum of the Bulgarian Communist Party (BCP) Central Committee,[4] which adopted the Theses; and (3) the joint party-state decrees of November 1967 on "increased profitability of the economy,"[5] which further detailed and elaborated the "new system." The major changes introduced by the drastically revamped 1968 blueprint will then be delineated, mainly on the basis of the decisions of the July 1968 Plenum of the BCP Central Committee[6] and the government decree of November 6, 1968, on the "gradual application and further development of the new system of management."[7] (These sources will hereafter be referred to in abbreviated form without further footnote documentation.) Finally, there will be a concluding overall assessment of the current status of and the prospects for the Bulgarian reforms.

The First Reform: A Thrust Forward

The "New System of Planning and Management of the National Economy" outlined in the December 1965 Theses was intended to cope with an array of interrelated problems characteristic of a Soviet-type command economy. These were broadly identified as excessive centralization of planning and direction, the stifling of enterprise autonomy and efficiency, deficiencies in motivation and material incentives, arbitrariness in price formation, and the general inadequacy of existing criteria of success for the purpose of measuring enterprise performance and spurring production units to supply desired output. Let us proceed, then, to examine the proposed remedies and their implementation—or lack of it—prior to 1968, in a number of specific areas: Planning in general, the role of the enterprise, capital investments, wages, taxing, pricing, agriculture and foreign trade.

Planning

Despite occasional hints and some isolated statements to the contrary, *the institution and role of central planning were never seriously questioned*, nor was "decentralization," as opposed to central planning, considered an official desideratum. In this respect, the Theses went farthest in their "liberalizing" provisions ("improved planning from below" and reduction of the number of obligatory indices), but even they—and, still more so, the decisions of the April 1966 Plenum which approved them—made it clear that "planning is a necessity" and that "the elimination of centralized management would be contrary to the socialist order." The avowed goal of the regime was a limited one: namely, to "combine centralism with increased independence for the enterprise" (Theses) so as to allow for greater flexibility.

The reference in the Theses to "improved planning from below," taken by itself, sounded as if it foreshadowed a significant decentralization of planning, inasmuch as it could have been interpreted to mean that great weight would be given in the formulation of the overall economic plan to the "contractual obligations" of individual enterprises, i.e., to the terms of the contracts negotiated directly, and presumably freely, between individual enterprises—since outright plan assignments to enterprises were to be abolished.

Under the contract system envisaged in the Theses, enterprises were to be permitted to plan their own production targets and submit them to the appropriate superior economic association or trust (and ultimately the central authority) for approval. Veto by the center, however, was meant to be exceptional. Yet this was not the case, since the Theses themselves specificied that the planning from below was to be based on "improved coordination, regulation, and guidance on the part of central planning." The enterprises' supposed freedom to contract thus became a largely meaningless postulate, especially when the April 1966 Plenum required them to meet "state orders" *(durzhavni poruchki)*—hardly any different from full-fledged plan assignments—for items of "decisive importance." The Plenum also imposed a series of obligatory ceilings and norms and made most contracts subject to approval from above, which in effect left the enterprise free to plan production only of items of minor importance. Symptomatically perhaps, the Plenum made no further reference to "planning from below," and the words "of planning" were dropped from the official designation of the "new system" in 1966.

Another planning reform affected the number of centrally-determined compulsory indices. The Theses specifically mentioned such indices only for the "volume of basic commodity production in real (physical) terms," limits (obligatory ceilings) on capital investments," "limits on basic raw and other materials," and "limits on foreign exchange." If this meant that compulsory indices would be limited to just these four categories, it would have shown the leadership's intention to move away from detailed central planning and direction—even though the retention of the notorious index for "volume of basic production in physical terms" would then have indicated, in the most charitable interpretation, an incomplete understanding of the centralizing tendencies inherent in the use of that index. However, the evidence indicates that there was no such intention. For instance, G. Filipov, then Deputy Chairman of the State Planning Committee, had already indicated in 1964 that many more than the four indices just mentioned would continue to be centrally determined, including quality and assortment as well as product and factor prices,[8] and B. Minkovski, editor of the foreign trade magazine *Vunshna Turgoviya*, had intimated that central planning "will even be increased, without in any way relaxing the state management of the economy."[9] At the Ninth Party Congress almost a full year after the Theses had been made public, Premier and party First Secretary Todor Zhivkov himself admitted that "no new methods of planning have yet been worked out."[10]

All this leaves the impression that the Bulgarian economy, the 1965 reform blueprint notwithstanding, remained essentially a centralized, command economy. What seemed like a move toward decentralization was actually a mere reshuffling of the chain of command whereby increased reliance was placed on the "branch principle" and on the previously-established economic associations or trusts *(stopanski obedineniya)*, which were to serve as intermediary bodies between the branch ministries and the enterprises under their jurisdiction. However, the trusts, which Zhivkov described at the

Ninth Party Congress as "basic forms of efficient economic management,"[11] gave rise to problems of monopolization and conflict with other decision-making bodies—problems that could not remain unnoticed. With regard to the former, the regime vacillated between threats of countermeasures against "negative monopolistic trends" (April 1966 Plenum) and rationalizations that monopolies under socialism "do not have the same disadvantages as under capitalism" (Ninth Congress). Meanwhile, jurisdictional conflicts led to repeated and often contradictory attempts to delineate areas of competence, with the regime first enlarging the rights of the branch ministries (April 1966 Plenum) and a year later those of the trusts[12]—but hardly ever those of the individual enterprise. As late as 1967, the trusts were still being characterized as "powerful agencies of state management,"[13] and any meaningful planning autonomy for the enterprise was still lacking.

The Role of the Enterprise

Given the retention of a substantial degree of centralized planning and direction of the economy, the principles of enterprise autonomy, self-support, profit-seeking, and democratization proclaimed in the Theses as desiderata of the "new system" needed greater backing both in theory and in practice than they actually received if they were to bring about the expected benefits of greater economic efficiency.

The Theses charged the individual enterprise with "producing net income for itself and for the state," thus making profitability (the ratio of profit to total capital) the general criterion of economic success. However, the enterprise was supposed to achieve this task on the basis of minimal freedom to enter into contractual agreements; it was permitted to manipulate only the prices of obviously minor production items; and it was compelled to relate premium payments to workers, above a guaranteed wage, to its profits after subtracting taxes and mandatory contributions to several enterprise funds. In addition, it was burdened with obtaining more, and possibly all, of its own investment funds out of profits and bank loans. This was at best a difficult assignment to accomplish within the contraints of the existing pricing and allocation system. In fact, "self-support" most probably remained a desideratum. From available indications, it appears to have met with some success in agriculture—assuming that collective farm income was correctly reported—but "planned losses" and subsidies continued in industry.[14]

Before going on to discuss some of the more specific aspects of the reforms as they affected the industrial enterprise, mention should be made of the "production committees" which had previously been established in industry as a step toward the regime's announced "democratization" of enterprise management.[15] The 1965 Theses entrusted these elective bodies with participation in some hitherto precluded areas, such as the "correct distribution of profits" and the "selection of managing cadres," but the committees were hardly meant to impair the decision-making power of the enterprise director. As Deputy Chairman Filipov of the State Planning Committee emphasized in 1964, the director remained the "representative of the state" in the enterprise, and the enterprises were "state property and did not belong to the workers' collective."[16] Moreover, workers' representatives made up only half the membership of the production committees' executive organs, the other half consisting of the director, the trade union chairman, the party secretary, and other *ex officio* members. The April 1966 Plenum ruled that decisions by the production committees were to be binding "if not contrary to the law," but if failed to redefine the areas of their competence. In any event, the committees remained merely advisory bodies rather than becoming real organs of worker participation in managerial decision-making.

Investments

A consistent theme of the reforms was the substitution of internal and credit financing of enterprise capital investments in place of the old system of state allocations of free capital. To this end, each individual enterprise was required to build up its own "expansion and technical improvement fund," the size of which was to be determined by a formula based on a percentage of existing enterprise capital, depreciation, and profits, to be deposited in the State Bank at interest. The formula varied for different branches of industry and tended to favor enterprises in the high-priority sectors. Bank loans to enterprises were to be repayable and interest-bearing, with highly differentiated rates of interest inversely related to the success of the enterprise—the higher the profitability, the lower the interest charge.[17] While designed to reward profitable enterprises, this provision tended to discourage bank borrowing by less successful enterprises, thus running counter to one of the goals of the regime. The 1967 Decree on Profitability also introduced some interesting competitive features in enterprise borrowing and repayment of bank loans—particularly, a provision permitting consumer goods producers to repay part of their bank loans used for the purchase of new equipment out of turnover tax assessments on the goods produced by that equipment. These features were intended to stimulate profit-seeking and consumer goods production.

But most investment projects were to remain centrally determined because of the still large investment needs of the state.[18] Moreover, the state was to continue to finance investments in priority sectors, especially in heavy industry where most of the unprofitable enterprises were to be found, thus eschewing the quest for internal or credit financing and profitability. In fact, as late as 1967, only 10 percent of total capital investments was reported to be financed by bank loans, although the "new economic system," according to the Decree on Profitability, had been applied to 70 percent of industry.

To provide greater incentive for efficient capital utilization, enterprises were permitted to retain a larger percentage of their depreciation allowances than before, and were required at the same time to pay a 6 percent interest charge on both fixed and working capital. However, the absence of any specification as to the method of capital valuation created problems, especially in view of the still prevalent practice of undervaluing capital and thus favoring the capital-intensive branches of industry. In sum, the pre-1968 reform blueprint, insofar as it related to capital formation and use, tended to remedy some of the most obvious obstacles to economic efficiency, but it still left enough—sometimes counterproductive—"levers" in the hands of the state to confront the enterprise with complex and difficult problems to overcome if it was to be profitable, let alone increase wages.

Wages

A significant innovation of the reforms was the scheme outlined in the Theses for tying part of wages and salaries to the profitability of the enterprise so as to stimulate "material interest." The enterprise "wage fund," consisting of the residual after subtracting non-labor costs, taxes, and internal fund allocations from receipts, was to be used, first, for the payment of basic wages conforming "on the average" to centrally-determined "guaranteed" wage scales, but not below a prescribed minimum (fixed relatively higher for workers than for employees), and second, for supplementary payments to workers and employees based on both collective and individual performance, including length of service. A "wage fund reserve," fixed as a percentage of the wage fund proper, was to serve as an emergency source for meeting minimum wages. These provisions of the Theses were, however, restricted to some extent by the April 1966 Plenum and considerably modified by the 1967 Decree on Profitability. The latter, in particular, stressed the need for a changeover to hourly wages (to be based on "machine-hours" in mechanized industries) and for the introduction of "multifactoral" (mnogofaktorni) wage criteria—i.e., quality of product, profitability, efficient use of capital, savings, labor discipline, and length of service. Of these criteria, the enterprise was supposed to have the right to select and apply those most appropriate to its particular line of production.[19] (Actually, the choice of criteria continued to be determined by higher authority, such as the economic trusts and the Labor and Wage Committee.) At the same time, the decree called for a wholesale revision of production standards and labor norms, as well as for salary cuts in cases of unsuccessful management, and for tighter rules tying enterprise wage funds to performance.

Considering that simple piece-rates were still in effect for about half of the country's industrial workers,[20] there was much to be said for the general application of hourly wages, as well as for an adjustment of labor norms and the adoption of more comprehensive wage-determining criteria. However, the regime's attempt to move simultaneously in diverse directions without any clarity of method only served to render the entire wage system more complicated and arbitrary, if not downright chaotic. Morever, the earlier revisions of labor norms had usually been at the expense of the workers' income, and the tying of wages to the productivity of enterprise capital introduced a factor extraneous to the workers' personal effort, which might operate to stifle rather than encourage labor initiative. It should be recalled that at the time of the Decree on Profitability was enacted, machines were being used in Bulgarian industry "at a bare 45-50 percent of capacity," according to Labor and Wage Committee Chairman M. Mishev.[21] Seen in that light, the decree's provisions appear to reflect more of a haphazard attempt to deal with multiple problems than a well thought-out and viable set of solutions.

Taxes

The reforms in the tax system were also supposedly designed to stimulate profitability, but in fact they tended to dampen material incentives. As the major source of state revenue, the 1965 Theses provided for still more sharply differentiated turnover taxes than already existed, as well as for a tax (really interest) on enterprise total capital. The most novel feature, however, was a "progressive income profits tax" on enterprises, which had the contradictory aims of promoting incentive and at the same time controlling undue increases in profits and wages. At the April 1966 Plenum, Premier Zhivkov admitted the self-defeating nature of this tax and called for its modification so as to combine progressive with proportional rates and to limit its application to enterprise net income.

Prices

The 1965 reform blueprint took what seemed to be a relatively promising approach to the crux of any meaningful economic reform—revision of the pricing system. After affirming the general principle that prices should be brought closer to "socially necessary labor costs" and made more flexible, the Theses called for the establishment of three different categories of prices: (1) those which the state would continue to set at fixed levels (primarily for capital goods and consumer necessities); (2) those for which the state would set only minimum and/or maximum limits between which prices could vary (applicable to most remaining goods produced under contracts between individual enterprises); and (3) those to be left free to fluctuate according to market conditions (presumably affecting seasonal and local items).

This hopeful start was belied, however, by repeated postponements of action to implement the price reform and by the introduction of various qualifications to the original blueprint. Even the Theses themselves contained a somewhat contradictory proviso that prices should be set in accordance with average industry costs (rather than actual enterprise costs) and, in October 1967, S. Dulbokov, chief of the party's Planning and Finance Department, stated that "prices should not diverge from the interests of the state."[22] The April 1966 Plenum and the 1967 Decree on Profitability both reiterated the promise of price reform, stressing the need for realistic and flexible prices and for a greater differentiation of factory and retail prices. Nevertheless, less and less was heard about the proposed "maximum-minimum limit" and free-market price categories envisaged in the Theses, and evidence strongly suggests that the old price system remained largely unchanged.

Agriculture and Foreign Trade

Substantial reforms had already been instituted in the sagging agricultural sector of the economy prior to the 1965 Theses.

Although space does not permit detailed discussion of these measures, suffice it to note that they included a number of steps to bolster incentives in agriculture—e.g., establishment of guaranteed minimum wages for collective farmers, pensions, production premiums, and encouragement of private plots—to which the Theses added the concept of differential land rents. The "new system" in agriculture further aimed at some reduction of centrally-determined compulsory production indices (which nevertheless remained substantial) and at tying collective farmers' incomes more closely to production results by relying on piecework rates *(akord)* as the basis for individual remuneration. (Collective farm chairmen and other salaried employees were to have only 70 percent of their salary guaranteed.[23]) Subsequent to the reforms referred to above, there were some contradictory attempts to narrow the gap between the agricultural collectives on the one hand and industry (and the state farms) on the other through the establishment of various collective-farm funds which intended to infringe upon the legal autonomy of the collectives, elimination of the theoretical claim to rent payments, and the imposition of limitations on the size and use of private plots under the new collective-farm Model Statute of March 1967.[24]

Finally, the reforms barely touched on matters involving foreign trade except for an announced revision of customs duties, a vague reference to the possibility of direct contacts between Bulgarian economic trusts and foreign enterprises "if necessary" and subject to central government control, and repeated exhortations to producers to make exports more competitive in international markets. Generally speaking, in this area, state monopoly and rigid command were to remain the rule.

In sum, the Bulgarian blueprint of economic reform as it evolved up until 1968 was a conglomerate of some worthwhile remedies, some questionable and contradictory measures, and a patchwork of undertakings aimed at improving, if not at radically altering, the existing system of centralized economic planning and command. Although deeds often did not jibe with words and implementation of the reforms was slow and piecemeal, *there nevertheless seemed to be a continuing, albeit hesitant, thrust forward through 1967*, and the pronouncements of the regime remained, on balance, in favor of applying the already toned down version of the original 1965 blueprint sooner or later.

The Second Reform: A Thrust Backward

In 1968, however, the blueprint itself was so drastically altered that, in effect, it no longer called for advance, but instead for retreat. The reversal was signaled by the decisions of the July 1968 Central Committee Plenum and confirmed by the ironically-titled "Decree on the Gradual Application and Further Development of the New System of Management of the Economy" of November 1968, which set January 1, 1969 as the deadline for total implementation of the "new" (read: modified) system. While several provisions of the pre-1968 blueprint were left unchanged, the overall purport of the Plenum decisions and the decree was a decisive swing back toward the very system which the 1965 Theses had tried to reform. What motivated the reversal is hard to pinpoint, but it seems reasonable to speculate that the move may have been partly prompted by the regime's realization, in the light of the 1968 events in Czechoslovakia, that unduly liberalizing economic reforms might tend to undermine the political monopoly of the Communist Party and jeopardize Bulgaria's smooth relations with Moscow.

Whatever the explanation, the July 1968 Plenum, under the equivocal guise of perfecting the "new system," opted instead for a *restrengthening of central planning* and direction of the economy. Premier Zhivkov openly repudiated the 1965 concept of "planning from below" on the grounds that individual units "cannot have a comprehensive view of the economy" and that the "scientific-technological revolution" necessitated recentralization.[25] Filipov, who had in the meantime been promoted to the post of chairman of the "permanent Commission on the New System" and in July 1971 was made secretary of the Party's Central Committee, endorsed the Plenum's reversal of policy in an October 1968 statement reaffirming "the need for increased (central) planning as society develops."[26]

The decision to recentralize planning was reflected in the restoration of a full complement of centrally-determined compulsory indices, limits, and norms. In addition to the four compulsory indices specified in the Theses, the July Plenum included the volume of basic contract deliveries between enterprises, the maximum size of enterprise wage funds, basic technical assignments, and norms for internal enterprise funds, interest, taxes, and customs duties, among the items subject to central determination. The overall effect of these extensions was to render the distinction between state "orders" and the supposedly voluntary "contractual" obligations of enterprises even more tenuous than before, and to all but nullify the circumscribed autonomy still remaining to the individual enterprise.

Recentralization was also implicit in certain *organizational* changes decided upon by the Plenum. At first, a new Committee on Economic Coordination was established within the Council of Ministers and vested with broad powers to coordinate "planning from above," and since most contracts would henceforth be centrally determined for all practical purposes, it was decided to reestablish a Ministry of Supplies and State Reserves (which had existed once before, between 1953 and 1956) to be in charge of inter-industry supplies.

Later on, the Council of Ministers and its Planning Committee took over the reins within a newly reorganized structure of the state economic trusts. Thus, not only was the number of these trusts reduced drastically with an amendment to the November 1968 Decree, but their functions were expanded at the expense of the individual enterprises, which were to "lose their former legal and economic independence."[27] In fact, the enterprises were deprived of any of the pre-1968 (and even limited pre-1971) "economic freedoms" which were, instead, transferred, albeit in a restricted version, to the trusts. For example, profit—as an indicator of success—would apply to the trusts only (and would consider foreign-trade transactions as well), while the component enterprises would be judged on the basis of their fulfillment of the old and too familiar quantitative and qualitative, production and cost, targets; moreover, the enterprises would be deprived of their own investment funds and previously independently managed wage funds.[28]

In an attempt to keep this renewed centralism from appearing excessive, the July Plenum promised that the people's councils (governing bodies at regional, district and local levels) would be given a greater say regarding economic activities within their areas of jurisdiction, and also reiterated that both the economic trusts and individual enterprises would enjoy "greater independence." In fact, however, the recentralization of economic planning and direction meant that the role of the people's councils, as well as of the trusts and especially the enterprises, would henceforth affect merely the implementation, not the formulation, of central economic decisions.

On the crucial issue of *price reform*, the July Plenum reiterated that rationality and flexibility in pricing remained worthwhile goals, but it conspicuously failed to make any mention of the three-level price system projected in the 1965 Theses. Nor was any encouragement to be found in an October 1968 statement by Chairman Filipov of the Permanent Commission on the New System, who categorically declared that "the movement of prices will be centrally planned in the future."[29] There were, however, some moves to establish more rational prices in certain areas. In October, T. Vulchev, Chief of the Planning and Economics Department of the Ministry of Machine Building, announced a 17-percent increase in wholesale prices for the machine-building industry and a 34.1-percent increase for the electrical industry.[30] In November, the government also confirmed a long-promised, more comprehensive revision of industrial wholesale prices, as well as of agricultural and import prices and various "tariff" rates (affecting freight, power, etc.), although no details were disclosed.[31] But while these moves appeared to signify the government's desire to rationalize the price structure, there was no sign of any intent to revive the idea of permitting market forces to determine prices of even a restricted category of consumer goods. But even the July Plenum and the November 1968 decree, which codified the revised "new system of management" and reiterated the goals of enterprise self-support and profitability[32] were superseded by the Planning Decree of 1970 and made most other reform remnants—from greater reliance on internal financing and bank loans (coupled with subsidies of a "temporary character") and on tighter and repayable bank credit to the introduction of "uniform criteria," governing the internal funds of enterprises and their taxes—obsolete or partly applicable only to the economic trusts. The income (profits) tax is to be now computed before and not after borrowed capital charges have been paid, but after the tax on the production funds and contributions to the three internal funds have been deducted, although this method of determining the profits tax "remains complex and unresolved."[33]

In the area of income distribution, the "multifactoral" system of wage criteria is to be retained and even extended to a Reserve (bonus) Fund, including the formulation of "long term norms" which take into account technological changes; yet both wage funds are to be the responsibility of the trusts, not enterprises, ostensibly in order to avoid an undue increase in wages at the expense of investment savings.[34]

Workers' participation in enterprise affairs, already meager under the pre-1968 reform blueprint, also seems to have been curtailed. The new "rules" established by the November 1968 decree and further elaborated in February 1969 with regard to the operation of the former "production committees"—now renamed "economic committees"—enlarged the rights of the docile trade union organization and made the enterprise director committee chairman,[35] thus reducing the role of the workers' collective to the point where "poor representation" of the workers was officially acknowledged.[36]

In *agriculture*, the trend since 1968 has been toward aping the organizational structure and methods of industry through the adoption of new forms of horizontal and vertical integration, such as "agricultural-industrial complexes" averaging 10,000 acres, and including about 75 percent of the arable land and working peasants, or so-called "industrial-farm conglomerates,"[37] through the establishment of "district trusts" of state forms, and through greater assimilation of collective and state farms, making the income of collective farm members and state farm workers over and above 90 percent of the basic rates dependent on profitability.[38] These measures, some of which are reminiscent of the pre-reform period, raise familiar questions regarding the efficiency and viability of mammoth-size farms and "agrogorod"-type units. In any event, it is in the agricultural sector that the greatest changes are currently taken place—perhaps as a result of the sharp decline (reported variably as 7.2 and 8.7-percent) in gross agricultural output in 1968, only partially remedied by an average 3 percent recovery in 1969 and 1970.[39] Whether or not, and to what degree, the recent measures toward integration and specialization will be successful remains to be seen.

In the field of *foreign trade*, the effect of the policy reversal signaled by the July 1968 Plenum made itself felt in the form of legislative measures enacted in November 1968 and June 1969 to restrict direct dealings between Bulgarian economic trusts and foreign enterprises,[40] which had apparently been permitted experimentally under the provisions of the 1965 Theses. These measures were followed by much more stringent action in November 1969 on the heels of Premier Zhivkov's disclosure of "gross violations of financial discipline" by the Merchant Fleet super-trust and its export-import department.[41] A new foreign trade law enacted shortly thereafter made it clear that no real autonomy would henceforth be permitted for any organization below the Foreign Trade Ministry.[42]

The Balance Sheet

In summary, then, Bulgaria in the 1960's has had not one, but two blueprints for economic reform. The pre-1968 blueprint, even though it never renounced central planning and management of the economy to any substantial degree, was nevertheless forward-looking in spirit and envisaged a number of liberalizing and rationalizing changes similar to those projected elsewhere in Eastern Europe. It should be stressed, however, that despite years of experimentation, "refinements," and often lively discussion, few of these features were actually implemented in practice, and where changes were made, they were often inadequately thought out, confusing, and counter-productive.[43] Premier Zhivkov himself stated at the July 1968 Plenum that "even today we lack the mechanism to implement some of the basic principles of the new system . . . and wherever the mechanism has been worked out, it has not yet been applied."[44] Still, until 1968, the provisions of the 1965 Theses were regarded as disiderata.

The 1968 blueprint, however, signaled a decisive swing away from the progressive features of the Theses. Centralized planning was to be expanded rather than narrowed; compulsory indices were to be increased, not reduced; and the idea of permitting some prices to be freely determined by market forces was in effect laid to rest. All that remained of the original blueprint was the stress of self-support, profitability and material incentives, to be implemented by price reforms from above and by expanded reliance on financial and fiscal controls wielded by central authority. And the regime remains substantially wedded to Stalinist-type economic priorities.

The official rationale for the 1968 economic model is the "objective necessity" to take advantage of the "scientific-technical revolution," which—according to Zhivkov's Report to the July 1968 Plenum—"makes it possible under socialist conditions to administer the economy in such a way as to prevent any break in the chain, to avoid duplication, and to reach full coordination of functions and activities among the individual units."[45] But "computerized" central planning hardly seems feasible in a technically backward society like Bulgaria's—at least for some time to come. Indeed, the Plenum itself indirectly recognized this when it called for a "unified information system" requiring "23,000 highly-skilled specialists by 1980"[46]—and even then it failed to discern the need for thousands more technicians of various types and the many kinds of sophisticated equipment required to run society in the electronic age. Zhivkov's justification for the 1968 reversal therefore seems too unrealistic to be taken seriously.

It appears much more plausible that the explanation for the about-face lies in the reluctance of the regime to let the winds of change blow too hard for fear that, as in Czechoslovakia, they might possibly endanger the tight grip of the party over society. The proceedings of the July 1968 Plenum, as well as developments since then, have made it abundantly clear that the regime does not intend to let the primacy of the party be challenged even in the economic sphere.[47]

Returning to a theme mentioned at the beginning, one might argue that the relatively backward Bulgarian economy can better afford to proceed with the model of central planning and command than a more developed one, and that consequently the pressures for change are not serious enough to propel the regime toward economic liberalization. But while the costs and burdens of over-centralization are perhaps less obvious in the context of present Bulgarian economic conditions, they are nevertheless real and likely to gain in importance as the country attains a higher level of economic development.[48]

A final, brief and self-evident, comment on the question central to this symposium: Within the broad framework of congruence of the East European Communist economies, the Bulgarian system since 1968 has been moving back in both word and deed, toward the old "command" model (growing criticism and even ridicule is heaped on the Yugoslav and the Sik "market-socialist" varieties since the July Plenum)[49] and is eagerly pursuing a closer integration with the Soviet economy internationally. Thus, implementing a decision by the July 1968 Plenum to effect a closer "linking of our economy with that of the Soviet Union through specialization and cooperation in production," various steps have been taken since to expand the Soviet share in Bulgaria's total foreign trade to a whopping 60 percent in 1970; including a series of sweeping bilateral agreements in 1969 and 1970 and the coordination of the Sixth Five-Year Plan (1971-5) with that of the other Comecon countries, and especially with the Soviet Union.[50]

One cannot but conclude with almost a sense of futility the assessment of the economic reforms and of the congruence hypothesis as applied to Bulgaria, as the findings may be compressed in a nutshell:

"Bulgarian economic reforms?"—"Tempest in a teapot."

"Congruence?"—"Yes, but more than anything with the Soviet economy, as has been the case since the end of World War II."

Notes

1. Little has been published in the West on Bulgaria, in general, and on Bulgarian economic reforms, in particular. Some recent sources are: J.F. Brown, "Reforms in Bulgaria," *Problems of Communism*, May-June, 1966 and his *Bulgaria Under Communist Rule* (New York: Praeger, 1970); L.A.D. Dellin, "Bulgarian Economic Reform—Advance and Retreat," *Problems of Communism*, October-September 1970 (an abbreviated version of the original paper for this symposium), his "Economic Reforms—An Assessment," *Review* (Brazil), July 1970 and "Bulgaria under Soviet Leadership," *Current History*, May 1963; Wolfgang Eggers, "Wirtschaftsreformen in Bulgarien" (Economic Reforms in Bulgaria), in K.C. Thalheim and H.H.

Hoehmann, eds., *Wirtschaftsreformen in Osteuropa* (Economic Reforms in Eastern Europe) (Cologne: Wissenschaft und Politik, 1968); Iwan Rankoff, "Wesen und Entwicklung der Wirtschaftsordnung Bulgariens" (The Nature and Development of the Bulgarian Economic System), in *Hamburger Jahrbuch fuer Wirtschafts- und Gesellschaftspolitik*, vol. 14, 1969; and Todor Zotschew, "Wandel und Wachstum der bulgarischen Volkswirtschaft" (Change and Growth in the Bulgarian National Economy), in *Bulgarische Jahrbuecher*, vol. 1, 1968. Valuable information and occasional analyses are found in Radio Free Europe Research, *Reports on Bulgaria*, especially Harry Trend, "Bulgaria's Economic Reform: Summary," December 14, 1965; Henry Schaefer, "Zhivkov's Great Society," September 23, 1968; R.N., "Organizational Experiments in Bulgarian Agriculture, March 27, 1969; and Steve Larrabee, "Bulgaria in the Technetronic Age," August 27, 1970.

2. Among the major domestic problems of the early 1960s were the agricultural stagnation and the resulting decline in overall growth rates, from 11.6 percent in 1955-1960 to 9.6 percent in 1961-1965 in gross social product, and from 9.6 to 6.7 percent in national income. Exports accounted for about twenty percent of national income, and eighty percent of them were agricultural products or industrial goods of agricultural origin. (See *Rabotnichesko Delo*, Oct. 31, 1967.)

3. "Draft Theses of the Politburo of the Bulgarian Communist Party on the New System of Planning and Management of the National Economy," (hereafter abbreviated as Theses), *Rabotnichesko Delo*, Dec. 4, 1965.

4. "Plenum of the Central Committee of the Bulgarian Communist Party: Report and Decisions" (hereafter, April 1966 Plenum), in ibid., April 29, 1966.

5. "Decree of the Central Committee of the Bulgarian Communist Party and the Council of Ministers of the People's Republic of Bulgaria on Increased Profitability of the Economy," (hereafter, Decree on Profitability), *Durzhaven Vestnik*, Nov. 10, 1967.

6. "Plenum of the Central Committee of the Bulgarian Communist Party, July 24-26, 1968: Report, Discussions and Decisions" (hereafter, July 1968 Plenum), *Rabotnichesko Delo*, July 25-27, 1968.

7. "Decree No. 50 of the Council of Ministers, November 6, 1968, on the Gradual Application and Further Development of the New System of Management of the National Economy" (hereafter, November 1968 Decree), *Durzhaven Vestnik*, Nov. 15, 1968, amended in ibid., June 6, 1969 and supplemented by the "Decree on Planning" of November 20, 1970, ibid. December 11.

8. Cited by F. Barbieri in the Belgrade *Politika*, Oct. 15 and 18, 1964 (translated in Radio Free Europe Research, *Bulgarian Press Survey*, No. 552).

9. *Vunchna Turgoviya*, December 1964.

10. Proceedings of the Ninth Congress, reported in *Rabotnichesko Delo*, Nov. 14-20, 1966.

11. Ibid.

12. D. Davidov, Deputy Chairman of the Labor and Wage Committee, writing in *Trud*, Oct. 7, 1967.

13. Ibid.

14. G. Filipov, in *Novo Vreme*, October 1968.

15. The production committees were initially established by the May 1963 Central Committee Plenum (see *Rabotnichesko Delo*, May 19, 1963). "Temporary Rules on the Composition and Functions of the Production Committees" were approved on April 15, 1965. (See *Partien Zhivot*, no. 7, 1965.)

16. Loc. cit. supra (n. 8).

17. November 1967 Decree on Profitability; also, statement by State Bank Director K. Nestorov, *Radio Sofia*, November 22, 1967 (cited in Radio Free Europe Research Report, *Bulgaria*, December 12, 1967).

18. Filipov, loc. cit. supra (n. 8).

19. According to Deputy Chairman A. Chaushev of the Labor and Wage Committee, an enterprise would have to apply at least one or two of the criteria. See *Otechestven Front*, Nov. 11, 1967.

20. Ibid.

21. *Trud*, Oct. 31, 1967.

22. *Rabotnichesko Delo*, Oct. 31, 1967.

23. Statement by Deputy Chairman S. Syulemezov of the State Planning Committee, in *Kooperativno Delo*, Dec. 5, 1965.

24. The Model Statute was approved by the Congress of Cooperative Labor Farms, March 28-30, 1967. For full text, see *Durzhaven Vestnik*, Feb. 28, 1968.

25. Loc. cit. supra (n. 5). See also Henry Schaefer, "Zhivkov's Great Society," *Radio Free Europe Research*, September 23, 1968.

26. *Novo Vreme*, no. 10, 1968.

27. The new legislation, "Decree on Planning," of November 20, 1970 in *Durzhaven Vestnik*, Dec. 11, 1970. The number of the trusts was reduced from 120 to 65 as of January 1970. Cf. also Steve Larrabee, "The Reorganization of the State Economic Association in Bulgaria," *Radio Free Europe Research*, February 1, 1971.

28. Beyond the above cited legislation, cf. G. Zhelev, deputy chief of the economic planning department of the party Central Commit-

tee, "Improving the Economic Mechanism of the Management of the National Economy," *Planovo Stopanstvo*, no. 3, 1971.

29. Loc. cit. supra (n. 26).

30. *Ikonomichesko Zhivot*, Oct. 3, 1968.

31. *Durzhaven Vestnik*, Nov. 5, 1968. Referring to this revision, allegedly introduced in 1971, a high party official warned that there will be "substantial price corrections in the course of the next five-year plan" (loc. cit. supra, n. 28).

32. This decree included four sets of "rules" covering economic trusts, state enterprises, foreign trade, and wages; and ten "ordinances" dealing with planning, profits, enterprise funds, contracts, budget contributions, enterprise-bank relations, purchase and sale of farm output, enterprise mergers and pricing of joint supplies, distribution of products and services among enterprises, and internal cost-accounting.

33. Zhelev, cited supra, n. 28.

34. Ibid.

35. See *Durzhaven Vestnik*, Nov. 15, 1968, and Feb. 7, 1969. Probably to prevent repercussions of the Polish workers' unrest, Zhivkov exhorted the unions "to protect the vital interests of the working people." (*Rabotnichesko Delo*, April 21, 1971).

36. *Trud*, June 7, 1969 and *Radio Sofia*, October 20, 1971.

37. *Ikonomicheski Zhivot*, Nov. 10, 1971. This trend was "codified" by the April 1970 Central Committee Plenum (see *Rabotnichesko Delo*, April 29-30, 1970) and by the regulations of 1970 (*Kooperativno Selo*, Oct. 27).

38. The latter measures were enacted in a February 1969 decree. See *Durzhaven Vestnik*, Feb. 25, 1969.

39. *Statisticheski Godishnik* (Statistical Yearbook) for 1970 and *Rabotnichesko Delo*, Jan. 25, 1970.

40. See *Durzhaven Vestnik*, Nov. 19, 1968, and June 6, 1969. Cf. also the author's "Political Factors in East-West Trade," *East Europe*, October 1969.

41. *Rabotnichesko Delo*, Nov. 5, 1969. These departments were to be dissolved in 1970.

42. Ibid., Nov. 21, 1969.

43. Illustrative of the confusion are the results of a poll among practicing economists in Khaskhovo City, 53.5 percent of whom admitted having difficulty in understanding the directives of the new economic system, while 72 percent were unable to use mathematical methods (*Ikonomichiski Zhivot*, July 29, 1970).

44. Zhivkov's report to the Plenum, ibid., July 25, 1968. In late 1970 Zhivkov again announced the approval of the "basic principles

of the new economic mechanism of the new economic system" (*Durzhaven Vestnik*, Dec. 11, 1970), thus contradicting the official claim that the new system had been totally implemented; a year later it was reported that the long-term norms necessary for the planning process of the new mechanism had not yet been worked out (*Radio Sofia*, Oct. 20, 1971).

45. Ibid. The same theme was stressed again at the September 1969 Central Committee Plenum (*Rabotnichesko Delo*, Oct. 25, 1969). The Tenth Party Congress of 1971 reiterated the goal of a "scientific-technical revolution," aided by the new economic mechanism, yet without any conviction or specifics (cf. *Rabotnichesko Delo*, April 28, 1971); no unusual theoretical or practical discussions have since been reported.

46. *Rabotnichesko Delo*, July 27, 1968.

47. The uncompromising attitude of the BCP leadership and its insistence upon tighter central controls over all sectors of the economy have been stressed repeatedly by First Secretary Zhivkov since 1968 (see, for example, *Otechestven Front*, Jan. 20, 1970 and Michael Costello, "Economic Units Under Fire in Bulgaria," *Radio Free Europe Research*, December 3, 1969) and dramatized most recently at the 1971 Tenth Party Congress, which adopted a new Party Program and a new Constitution (texts in *Rabotnichesko Delo*, April 21-26 and May 9, 1971).

48. Results of the 1969 economic plan were disappointing, and more modest targets were set for 1970 and 1971; national income during 1966-1970 showed a further reduction in growth rates (cf. n. 2, supra), to 6.2 annually. (*Rabotnichesko Delo*, Nov. 20, 1969, Jan. 25, 1970, and Jan. 29, 1971.)

49. Cf., e.g., G. Filipov in *Novo Vreme*, no. 10, 1968.

50. *Rabotnichesko Delo*, March 10, 1971. See also my "Bulgaria," in R.F. Staar, ed., *Yearbook on International Communist Affairs*: 1971 (Stanford: Hoover Institution, 1971). "Integration" and "congruence" with the Soviet economy and bloc have been urged repeatedly by writers (e.g., G. Popisakov in *Novo Vreme*, no. 4, 1969) or party leaders (e.g., Politbureau member T. Tsolov in *Otechestven Front*, June 13, 1971); it has been a favorite topic by First Secretary Zhivkov himself, who exchanged the premiership for the newly established chairmanship of the State Council in July 1971. Also, according to the new Premier, Stanko Todorov: "The building of a developed socialist society in a country like Bulgaria . . . is possible only by progressive integration with the economies of other socialist countries, above all the Soviet Union" (*World Marxist Review*, June 1971, p. 41).

4

Czechoslovakia: Prohibitive Odds

Ota Sik

I

This paper will concentrate on the Czechoslovak concept of economic reform, that is, on the basic principles underlying the changes in the economic system of Czechoslovakia. I shall, therefore, omit the detailed historical development of the economic situation in our country, which I have treated elsewhere.[1]

The ideas behind the reforms in the system of planning and management—and, indeed, in the overall economic system of Czechoslovakia—derived from past experiences that facilitated our theoretical development. These earlier undertakings are rarely mentioned, which makes our theoretical development in recent years appear more spontaneous that it actually was.

In the first place, we accumulated important economic experience following the Second World War. In the immediate postwar years, an economic system was developed in Czechoslovakia that, even at that time, was consciously and purposely called a democratic economic system. It was a system that representatives of the various political parties helped to create. The most important contribution, however, was made by outstanding economists who were members of the communist party, such as Frejka, Frank, Goldman, Margolius, Loebl, Fabinger, Fukatko, and others. These economists knew, even at that time, that in a highly industrialized state like Czechoslovakia it would be difficult to organize a socialist economy by strictly following the Soviet model. I am afraid that these facts have not yet been sufficiently emphasized by economic historians, and I am sure they should be given much greater attention, because these men performed a great feat.

What took place in Czechoslovakia during the first few years, until about 1950-51, was the unfolding of a relatively new, progressive, and specific form of socialist economic development. In those years the enterprises—i.e., the large-scale nationalized enterprises—were developed to be market-oriented. They operated under rather diffi-

59

cult competitive conditions, both inside the country and on foreign markets. Actually, it was we who for the first time tried to combine the market with national economic planning. The first plan introduced in Czechoslovakia was a two-year macro-economic plan based on organizational and methodological principles quite different from those of the Soviet-type planning applied in Czechoslovakia later on.

Unfortunately, however, this development was too brief, as everyone knows. It was soon suppressed on the pretext that the so-called cold war had broken out. The purpose was to do away with any autonomous development in the so-called people's democracies; to enforce a pattern which was completely subordinated to the political and economic goals of Moscow; to impose structural changes that suited the political purposes of the Soviet Union at that time; and, generally, to introduce a political and economic system of management closely corresponding to the Soviet "model."[2]

The political premises for these fundamental changes, from which Czechoslovakia never really recovered, were the political trials of that period. The purpose of these trials in all of the people's democracies was to eliminate from the political leadership all those who developed creative, rational ways of thinking, and who had the courage to carry out forms of economic development appropriate to Czech conditions. All the persons I quoted above were arrested: the majority of them were executed or imprisoned for years. In their stead, men were to be elevated to political leadership who conformed to Soviet power politics, and who would completely submit to it.

The second experience, all too easily forgotten, was the reorganization of planning and management that took place in Czechoslovakia during 1957-58. As early as 1956, it was recognized that the Czechoslovak economy was lagging behind in technological progress, that it was becoming more and more ineffective, that the extensive sources for growth were being exhausted, and that new forms of management were necessary if development was to take a favorable turn.

At that time certain rudimentary ideas and concepts of reform developed quite spontaneously in Czechoslovakia. A similar development of reform concepts was observed almost simultaneously, yet quite independent of the Czech situation, in the Soviet Union, particularly under the influence of Liberman's writings. I emphasize this because it is not sufficiently known that, when Liberman could do little more than theorize, we in Czechoslovakia had already tried to put into practice similar ideas of our own. Our aim was to restrict the scope of command planning, to reduce the number of compulsory indicators, and to make the enterprises more independent and more profit-conscious in order to develop certain criteria of efficiency. Independently of Liberman, we proposed to let the enterprises share in planned profits by distributing bonuses, so as to induce them to help increase profits. An attempt was even made to achieve growth and more efficient development by trying to avoid dictating plans from above. Instead, a norm was established giving a higher bonus rate to enterprises adopting and fulfilling an ambitious plan than to those adopting a "softer" plan (the usual practice in the past) and then overfulfilling it by a large margin. This was an attempt to induce enterprises to formulate more realistic plans. Unfortunately, as was the case with later economic reforms in many other socialist countries, the effort to create an interest in more efficient development was not backed with the courage to do away with command planning. To my mind, this is also the gist of Liberman's theory.

The fear of abolishing command planning altogether at that time had, of course, its ideological reasons, because command planning was looked upon as an axiom of the socialist economy and society. An attack against command planning was considered to be an attack against socialism in general. This was the reason for choosing a compromise solution which, on the whole, proved unsuccessful. The first year of its application showed some increased initiative by the enterprises, but by 1959-60 it had become clear that the compromise could not survive, and that the old features of command planning suppressed any initiative shown by the production units.

The reaction to these difficulties was typical of the Novotny regime. In 1961, the Third Five-Year Plan was not fulfilled. Despite all the attempts to introduce some innovations, the plan was set up in such a way that its fulfillment in the production and investment sectors proved impossible. Extensive resources were practically exhausted. Therefore, the authorities hoped to increase the volume of production by prescribing high targets in productivity growth, although the enterprises lacked the concrete technical and technological preconditions. As a result, almost all branches of industry failed to meet productivity targets and met only one-half of the planned investment targets. This caused the elimination of many expected capital projects during the first year alone. There followed a complete breakdown of the Third Five-Year Plan, which was then quietly laid to rest.

Novotny sought the cause for the breakdown in what he called the decentralization process. What he really blamed was the reorganization of 1957-58, making it responsible for the ensuing difficulties. Actually it was the other way around. Nevertheless, there was an immense new wave of centralization and a strengthening of command planning in 1962. I emphasize this because the very same process is repeating itself today, even though a great deal of historical experience would counsel against it. As a result, the Czechoslovak economy broke down in 1963, with total production and the national income declining even in absolute terms. Czechoslovakia was also the only industrial state after the Second World War where real—and not only nominal—wages declined in absolute terms.[3]

Only because of this catastrophe were we able to press our new reform ideas and to show that it was not decentralization that was to blame but rather the earlier half-hearted compromise on reform. In framing our own concept for reform on the basis of years of preparatory theoretical study, we tried to analyze, synthesize, and perfect all these earlier experiences and to encompass them in a new theory.

II

The essential truth we were brought to realize at that time was that a socialist economy cannot develop optimally if command planning of whatever kind is continued. We realized that no central agency is able to discern the complicated interrelationships among the four basic aspects of socially necessary economic development, nor is it able to take them into account in its plans and to create optimum conditions in the enterprises. Let me emphasize that we did not arrive at these theoretical conclusions by a deductive method, but by inductive analytical work, on the basis of which we made certain theoretical generalizations. We showed that production must develop: (1) in volume; (2) by quantitative growth, adjusting to a continually-changing structure; (3) by changing and improving its quality (i.e., considering the utility effects); and (4) with a steady growth in productivity and effectiveness.

These four basic processes are mutually dependent in a very complicated way in each branch, in each enterprise, at each moment; and assume ever-changing concrete forms. In every single enterprise, in every branch, and at every moment, it is necessary to shape and relate the volume of production to the development of quality (utility), of costs, and of general structure. These must be constantly revised and harmonized in each line of production. The center by itself is unable to discover these complicated quantitative relationships. It possesses neither the necessary expert knowledge of production nor the necessary knowledge of concrete needs. If the center really were in a position to understand all these relationships—at every moment, for each branch, and for each enterprise—there would be no need for enterprise management. That, of course, is an entirely abstract and utterly impossible idea.

The center would have to depend on information from the enterprises concerning the proper development of these four related processes. I emphasize this, because, to my mind, these complicated relationships are ignored by those who believe that optimum development of a socialist economy might be assured from the center with the help of a giant computer system. Such a computer system is currently regarded especially in the Soviet Union, the German Democratic Republic, and once again in Czechoslovakia, as the most progressive socialist system of our time. Attempts are made to prove that, up to the present, technical difficulties alone have precluded an optimal development of a socialist economy. I am convinced that the center cannot find optimal solutions for the individual branches and enterprises even with the help of the most complicated computer system; for such a system can only work on the basis of data fed into it by the enterprises.

Here I come to other basic points, those of material incentives and competitive pressure. In the current stage of socialist development, a stage that will continue for some time (I mean that the desired stage of communism is still a long way off), people will change their methods of work only if they expect to derive certain economic advantages from the change. (This is, of course, a Marxist principle that is disregarded today.) Therefore, without some economic advantage or pressure, the enterprises will neither increase the quantity of production, nor improve its quality, nor will they change the structure of output or reduce production costs, let alone aim at an optimum development of the four basic aspects of socially-necessary economic progress. Every one knows, of course, that production in Western countries would begin to stagnate if material inducement and economic pressure were to disappear. Experience proves that the center is simply unable to provide an incentive for an optimum solution because it is not in a position to tell which solution would be the optimum one. And the enterprise will not indicate to the center the possibilities for optimum changes so long as it is not forced to do so economically.

We in Czechoslovakia simply came to the conclusion that even in a socialist economy the market, with its real competitive pressures, cannot be replaced with anything else.

When we arrived at this theoretical conclusion, we knew that it would be considered unsocialistic. But we could not ignore our findings. We had seen that there were no partial solutions. We recognized that it was impossible to introduce partial improvements in command planning or to simply reduce the number of indicators and still achieve a truly optimal operation of the enterprises. We saw that all these compromise solutions had led nowhere. An optimal solution at the enterprise level is impossible so long as the enterprise receives from above even a single indicator that cannot be harmonized with all the other necessary aspects of development (such indicators could be, for example, the number of workers employed, the determination of investments, or the volume of priority goods). Even a minimal assignment of indicators from the center is an obstacle for an optimal solution and is contrary in principle to the solutions that the enterprises would have to find for themselves if they really began to produce for the market. As a result, it was decided to make a fundamental change in the system, whereby the discontinuation of command planning and a reintroduction of the economic function of the market would be secured.

It goes without saying that we were able to assert ourselves in Czechoslovakia thanks only to the disastrous economic situation in which the country found itself, and which was much worse than any other socialist country had ever experienced.[4] For quite definite reasons, all the difficulties in Czechoslovakia had become so compounded that the political leaders were completely lost and saw no alternative but to accept very revolutionary and fundamental proposals for reform, particularly because they were under immense social pressure from the enterprises themselves, where we had found much support from the very beginning.

III

Following is a brief summary of the recommended reforms:

(1) *In the first place, proposals were made for a fundamental change in the central management apparatus and in the organization of production generally.* It was necessary, first and foremost, to reduce the size of the giant bureaucratic apparatus that had been built up during the period of command planning. Czechoslovakia had at times as many as eighteen economic ministries, each with three, four, or five main departments—a bureaucratic apparatus that made any kind of economic reform quite impossible. This had already been recognized as a fundamental truth at the time when the reform proposals were officially accepted by the political leadership.[5] In spite of this official approval, the proposals were never implemented by the Novotny regime. I emphasize this fact because they were

consciously sabotaged by the apparatus from the very first month. One should really speak of a stillborn economic child, of a suffocated economic embryo.

We intended to do away with the large number of industrial ministries and go back to a single small industrial ministry alongside a few general economic ministries, such as are also known and necessary in Western countries, that is, a ministry of finance, a ministry of foreign trade, and a small administratively subordinated planning commission. The struggle to do away with the enormous bureaucratic apparatus was not easy; and here lies one of the social foundations for the strong political opposition of the bureaucrats to the reforms. This resistance was overcome by the entire people only during the Czechoslovak "Spring" of 1968. It is interesting to note that the number of ministries was being reduced during that period, and that *after* the intervention the reduction process was more or less completed. But this was accomplished in connection with the transition to the federative system, so that on balance the total apparatus had not become much smaller. Thus, while the large central apparatus was reduced in size, new bureaucracies were created in its stead in the two political subdivisions of the state, that is, in the Czech and the Slovak territories, so that the bureaucrats did not lose their jobs, and the whole administration is today more complicated than ever.

By reorganizing production, the enterprises were to be completely freed of state direction and regulation and were once more to become independent units in the market. This task was accomplished during the months of the Czechoslovak "Spring," but the trend was reversed after the Soviet intervention. Initially, the old command economy was not openly reintroduced, but central-plan assignments were imposed on the enterprises in a hidden form by way of so-called agreements between the center and the enterprises that were equivalent to orders imposed from above. Later on, the usual commands and compulsory targets of the central planning apparatus were openly reintroduced.

Our objective was to create genuine competition, which in fact was coming into existence when, unfortunately, it was nipped in the bud. Only the first steps had been taken, and time was too short to achieve more. The goal was to abolish monopolies that, in Czechoslovakia, yielded more absolute power than at any time before. Never in its development had capitalism known such monopoly power. As is known, every branch was actually equivalent to a single large corporation that developed not, of course, as a result of a genuine concentration of production, but as an administrative, pasted-together entity controlling innumerable enterprises which had nothing in common. It was paramount to break up this administrative structure, but, as I said, we did not succeed in doing so. We wished to make the enterprises independent and free to make their own decisions. A law on state enterprises was prepared that would have allowed them to decide by themselves whether they wished to remain together or to separate. They were to act only on the basis of prior calculations of the most effective economic alternative, information that no higher authority could possess.

Finally, we counted on far-reaching cooperation between Czechoslovak enterprises and advanced foreign companies. Through such cooperation—which was to go very far—we hoped to achieve rapid technological development and access to new markets, especially to third markets in cooperation with Western enterprises, etc. Of course, such cooperation has now been quietly eliminated and Czechoslovak enterprises no longer dare even make such suggestions.

Furthermore, our intention was to restore private enterprise in the service industries, as it became clear that in small industry, crafts, minor services, etc., there was no alternative to private initiative. As is probably known, private initiative did in fact assert itself illegally because the socialist communal enterprises were unable to satisfy the needs of the population. They were unable to do so because of the attitude of their own employees, who worked but achieved little all day, "saved" materials, and then continued their work at home in the evenings—but as private entrepreneurs. One had simply to legalize what was going on spontaneously so as not to continue depriving the state of the tax revenue it was losing when these small businesses were clandestine. Nowadays, people are again afraid to risk the opening of small private shops. They do not know how things will develop in the future, are suspicious, and convinced that it is better for them to carry on as usual.

(2) *The goal was to change the function of prices and of foreign trade.* We were convinced that it was impossible to go on without true "economic" prices, that is, prices that are initially formed on the basis of competitive production costs, and that deviate from production costs as a result of supply and demand. We were likewise convinced that one is unable to determine such economic prices centrally, by way of a command system. I emphasize this point once more because it was a matter of heated discussion with the economists of the German Democratic Republic, who spoke repeatedly of economic reform but absolutely refused to admit that this required a real market with truly economic prices.

We came to the conclusion that such economic prices could develop only in a real market and under the pressure of competition. The economists of the German Democratic Republic and a few economists from the USSR, especially members of the Fedorenko Institute, contended that a socialist price system could be developed whereby economic prices would be centrally calculated by using a comprehensive computer system. Thus far, however, nobody has been able to explain how this might be done in practice. For at least fifteen to twenty years (to my personal knowledge), economists have been telling us that work has been going on toward developing such a system, but that it has not yet been completed. Plotnikov, the Soviet economist, said much the same thing at a conference of the International Economic Association in Portugal in 1969.

I am firmly convinced that it is impossible to fix concrete economic prices at the center, that is, from above. In Czechoslovakia there are about 1.5 million concrete prices that in fact ought to be changed all the time. It is unnecessary to point out how complicated this matter is. But, after all, even if it were possible to calculate all the detailed relationships, the decisive element remains that the calculation should be made on the basis of information submitted by the enterprises themselves—information that the center is unable to control. The center cannot find out whether an enterprise could have cut the cost more or less than it reportedly did. The center cannot determine what technical or technological changes should have been made, unless the enterprise makes a correct report. The center is unable to judge what microstructural alterations would be necessary in the interest of the consumers if an enterprise chooses to cover them up. And the center is absolutely unable to appraise how the quality of a product might have been improved. All this makes it impossible for the center to arrive at a critical appraisal of the information submitted by the enterprises, so that truly economic prices cannot be determined from above.

This is the reason why we came to the conclusion that prices should be able to fluctuate about as freely as they do in the capitalist countries. Yet it was realized that one could not switch over to free prices overnight, because this would have led to galloping, uncontrollable inflation. Czechoslovakia has in fact been experiencing hidden inflation for some decades now, hidden behind administratively-controlled prices. Had these prices been unfrozen, nothing could have stopped their upward climb. This was why we attempted to introduce free prices very gradually *via* three price groups: a first group of centrally-fixed and controlled prices as before; a second group of "limit prices" (that is, prices allowed to fluctuate within prescribed limits); and a third group of free prices.

An attempt to accelerate the transition to economically justified prices by means of a price reform was made in 1966. I purposely mention this price reform because it failed, and its failure is now being used as an excuse for attacking all subsequent reforms. We tried at that time to achieve a rapid change in the so-called wholesale prices (that is, the prices at which enterprises make deliveries to one another and to the trade organizations) with the help of a computerized price reform. Without changing the wholesale prices, we would have been completely unable to begin work on the new system, because all price relations were administratively distorted. We had prices yielding high or low profits as well as loss prices, so that it was absolutely impossible to make effective calculations. The existing prices made it impossible for many enterprises to show even a minimum of necessary capital accumulation. Consequently, the thing to do was to establish prices assuring more or less uniform profitability. However, we indicated from the very beginning that one should not passively accept the information submitted by the enterprises without critical scrutiny. (I wish to point out that the intention was not to reform individual prices, but major price groups.) Considering the time element, the theoretical groundwork for the reform was not bad. We demonstrated how one should try to simulate the market; how, through comparative analyses, one could check the over-all information of the enterprise so as to detect gross speculation. However, this was not done. The price reform was carried out in a very simplified form, and I feel justified in saying that it was consciously sabotaged by the affected ministries. This was a procedure typical of the bureaucratic apparatus, for the ministries were the greatest enemies of the economic reforms. It was truly ironic, therefore, to entrust the ministries with the gradual introduction of reforms.

The price reform did not succeed, because prices were pushed up by the enterprises under the pretext of high costs, which led to excessive profits. Therefore, the desired economic pressure on the enterprises did not develop, and instead inflation accelerated still further. The unsuccessful price reform was later used as an argument against reforms in general, and attempts were made to discredit the entire process. But, it should be emphasized that even this less than successful price reform cannot be regarded as an obstacle to subsequent economic reforms. The new prices at least permitted the enterprises to become more independent, which would have been impossible under the old prices. Moreover, excessive profits could have been reduced by higher taxes—which in fact were introduced during the spring of 1968. Higher taxes would have placed the enterprises under the desired pressure, given time. Therefore, the price reform cannot be used as an argument against reforms in general, but rather as an argument against the centralized administrative determination of prices.

When speaking of price changes, one must add that we had no intention of changing all prices at the same time, by one single reform, but to alter them gradually. We reckoned with a transitional period of several years. We knew that a single fundamental change in retail prices would have been impossible—first, for social reasons, and second, because it would have caused economic chaos. The structure of demand would have been altered so radically that it would have been impossible to adjust production so as to keep up with it. We therefore envisaged a long transitional period, in the course of which we planned, first of all, to consolidate the various turnover taxes into taxes affecting broader price groups and, ultimately, into a single turnover tax. The great difference in turnover tax rates transpires from the fact that there were prices that carried no tax at all, while others were burdened with a turnover tax of several hundred percent. Of course, such prices could not but completely distort consumption. Often a very high tax would increase the price of products that would have had substantially increased sales at regular prices and whose production could have been easily expanded, since they were made of local raw materials. Conversely, prices of other products were kept low even though they were made of costly foreign raw materials, even though their production could not have been easily increased, and even though the demand for them could not have been satisfied for many years.

Along with the change in the turnover tax, a buyer's market was to be created gradually, and the necessary functions of the market were to be restored with the help of a purposeful central anti-inflationary policy: i.e., relative reduction of investment in heavy industry; higher interest rates; savings in the bureaucratic apparatus; tying wage increases to higher productivity; priority to consumer goods production, highly competitive export industries, services, and housing construction; gradual abolition of state subsidies, especially in the foreign trade sector; anti-monopolistic policies and promotion of competitive pressures, particularly via foreign trade, etc. Along with the growing pressure of competition within the individual branches of production, the groups of free prices and limited prices were to be correspondingly enlarged, and that of controlled prices restricted. Even during the transitional period, however, a market was to be simulated for some of the most important centrally-fixed prices (only for those where the utility effect could be determined), and pressure was to be exerted upon the production costs of the enterprise.

This, in broad outlines, was our concept concerning the reform of domestic prices in Czechoslovakia. It was, of course, necessary to make fundamental changes in the foreign trade sector as well. If one had to characterize the then existing foreign trade system in Czechoslovakia in a general way, one would identify it as an absolute state monopoly, the most comprehensive protectionist system possible. Our Czechoslovak system of foreign trade "protected" our total domestic production in a manner resulting in real losses to the population, greater than any known precedent. Frankly, it was impossible to figure out the exact magnitude of these losses because, in the first place, there were no rational price and monetary criteria to go by and, in the second place, all the data concerning foreign trade were strictly-kept secrets. However, on the basis of partial analyses, I think that I am justified in saying that these losses were such that it would be better not to speak to our workers about exploitation in the capitalist system.[6]

Suffice it here to recall that the domestic producers supplying the monopolistic foreign trade organizations with exportable goods at domestic prices knew nothing, indeed were supposed to know nothing, about the prices prevailing on world markets. That was a state secret. Nobody was supposed to know at what prices Czechoslovak goods were sold abroad. It was obvious, however, that the low quality, the technological backwardness, the excessively high production costs, etc., of our goods led to enormous losses that had to be covered by ever larger exports in order to pay for the original volume of imports. The increasing magnitude of these losses may be judged indirectly from the fact that, during the first post-war years, we obtained on the average one U.S. dollar against seven korunas worth of exports. Soon, however, we needed exports worth twice as much, and in 1967, we needed exports worth 31 korunas to earn the same dollar of foreign exchange.[7] Today, even 31 korunas are insufficient, and it is impossible even to guess at the black market exchange rates inside Czechoslovakia.

We not only failed to make a profit on an increasing number of our exports, but we were unable to recoup their cost in labor, or—in recent years—even the cost of raw materials, which often had to be imported. According to calculations made at the Economics Institute in Prague, raw materials were often re-exported at a loss after having been processed in our country. Thus, at the price actually realized from the sale abroad and converted at the official exchange rate, the producer had to be given a high state subsidy that in itself exceeded domestic profit, the wage cost, and some of the raw material cost. If we had not exported, a clear profit could have been made. But this was impossible under the circumstances, for then we would have been simply unable to pay for our imports. As a result, more goods had to be exported at a loss year after year. Let me emphasize that this practice continues now at a truly terrifying pace. It is the only way of keeping the balance of payments even. Trade with the West is so difficult that our foreign exchange reserves long ago dwindled to nothing, so that we must export at any cost in order to avoid insolvency.[8] Unfortunately, this fact was totally disregarded in the past and continues to be today. The foreign trade organizations simply do not care whether they operate at a profit or at a loss, for their main task is to fulfill the quantitative plan, that is, to export a certain volume of goods in order to assure the planned volume of imports. The volume of goods to be exported is simply increased year after year in order to match the desired volume of imports. The magnitude of the losses is compounded by the fact that the difference between the prices at which the state foreign trade organizations acquire domestic goods for export and those at which they resell imported goods to the domestic producers becomes greater every year. The purchasing of exportable goods from the Czechoslovak producers at domestic prices and selling imported goods to them at domestic (though gradually rising) prices, and the need to export larger and larger quantities year after year, makes the total cost of the exports always higher as compared to the imports. This represents rising losses that must be covered anonymously by the state budget. The foreign trade organizations are tied to the state budget, and their deficits are covered year after year through subsidies. This is truly a terrible system, and the population must be kept in the dark about it. I am certain that this is one of the reasons why foreign trade matters are a state secret, and why certain people were frightened at the very thought that state monopoly might be abolished. This would have brought to light certain machinations in the past that should never become known.

The only possible remedy was to create competition and decentralize foreign trade. In concrete terms, this meant paying domestic producers the price actually obtained in foreign markets and, secondly, allowing them to choose the most effective export and import channels. They were to be allowed to decide for themselves whether they wished to continue dealing with an existing or with a newly established foreign trade organization, or to export and import directly. This reform would have put all foreign trade organizations under competitive pressure. If we had done this suddenly, however, many of our producers would have gone bankrupt. They would have been unable to cover their costs from their exports. It was therefore necessary to subsidize these losses, at least for a while. We intended to recalculate the losses and to identify the individual producers in need of subsidies. The subsidies were to be temporary and gradually eliminated, according to plan. The time limit and the rate of reduction were to be differentiated by groups of products, but the producers had to know that the subsidy would be discontinued in, let us say, three, four, or five years. By that time, the enterprise was expected to become competitive and to live from its own earnings. It had to make the necessary structural, qualitative, and technological adjustments in order to become competitive.

We did begin with this important task. We had already allocated subsidies to specific groups of goods, but the foreign trade ministry—considering the existing balance-of-payments difficulties—was far more interested in increasing the volume of exports than in systematically reducing the size of the subsidies. As a result, the intended reforms were once again carried out in a haphazard manner, and producers were not put under pressure. Substantial foreign credits would have helped us bridge the temporary gap. But it was necessary that the aims and working methods of the foreign trade ministry be fundamentally changed.

Unfortunately, since 1968 all these goals have again been abandoned. Decentralization and de-monopolization have ceased. Producers no longer have freedom of choice in foreign trade. Compulsory export and import targets have been reintroduced; consequently, the intended economic pressure has completely disappeared.

In summary, we intended to create a real market, a market for commodities as well as for labor and capital, a market that, however, would have been subjected to macro-economic planning and direction.

(3) This brings us to the third point, that is, the *changes in planning and general economic policy*. In place of the former mandatory ("directive") planning, we intended to introduce macro-economic guideline ("indicative") planning. Basic and comprehensive social and economic plans were to be drawn up, taking into account different development alternatives ("variants"). These alternatives of development were to be formulated and appraised in a democratic manner. This point must be emphasized, because I am certain that as long as only a single bureaucratic planning center is responsible for the formulation of economic plans, and as long as democratic opportunities to judge and determine them are lacking, all attempts

to work out alternatives must fail, and even macro-economic plans cannot do proper justice to the interests of society. For this reason, the idea that several alternative plans of economic development must be worked out before choosing the optimum variant was inseparably connected to the idea of political democratization.[9]

Therefore, we reckoned quite concretely with the institutional establishment of a Central Economic Council, conceived, however, not as a bureaucratic apparatus, but as an arrangement of committees of experts (with a very small staff) put together in a democratic fashion and representing diverse and important interest groups among the population. These committees were to suggest various social and economic goals and to formulate different development alternatives. After appropriate technical computations and con-cretizations by the staff, the different alternatives were to be evaluated by Parliament after broad discussions in political and other mass organizations. One plan was then to be selected from among the various alternatives and finally adopted. However, this plan was not to be considered as binding, like the old plans, but was merely to serve as a macro-economic frame of reference for the enterprises. In brief, it was to assist the enterprises in their own long-term planning, but they had to make their own decisions at their own risk.

The plan as finally adopted was to have served as the basis for governmental economic policy. The government would have been bound to try and implement the established goals with the help of its instruments of economic policy, that is, with the help of its fiscal and monetary policies.

Investment policy was to occupy the most important role in influencing economic development. Our idea of investment policy was to have those investments lying outside the production sector, that is, mainly infrastructural investments, directly regulated and financed by the state. Investments in the production sector were to be only indirectly controlled by the state, primarily via its credit policy. We intended to submit to the banks a guideline figure from the macro-economic plan concerning the desired volume of credit. The volume of credit was to be divided into three large groups, namely, short-term, medium-term, and long-term credit, and their breakdown was also to be indicated to the banks by the planning center. On the basis of these guideline figures, the banks were to seek with the enterprises concrete credit relationships whereby competition would prevail; that is, the banks, operating within the framework of centrally controlled interest rates and maximum periods of loan repayment for the three credit groups, were to grant credits to those enterprises guaranteeing the most rapid and regular repayment of the loan.

Space does not permit a detailed discussion. Suffice it to say that we assigned an important role to credit policy as an indirect instrument for influencing economic development. Taxes being so high, the enterprises would have been unable to finance major investments from their own resources. They would have had to borrow money to pay for every major investment project, and so credit policy would have served as a possible steering wheel for the center. However, let me emphasize that this would not have meant a regimentation of enterprise investment activity by the center, for both the total credit volume and that of each of the three credit groups were meant only as guidelines that might have been exceeded or not, depending on the competitive relationships between banks and enterprises. The planning center would, of course, have been notified of the attainment or non-attainment of the guideline figure. This information would have been necessary in order for the center to keep an eye on anticipated macro-structural investment allocations, on anticipated investment effectiveness, etc. This knowledge is very important in forecasting other macro-economic processes and relationships and in improving long-term planning. Thus, our goal was not to subject the investment decisions of the individual enterprise to strict regimentation but—on the contrary—to try to attain long-term economic and social changes by a continual improvement of planning.

None of these fundamental changes in planning and controlling the economy were understood or implemented by the existing Planning Committee. Not even during the months of the Czechoslovak "Spring" were we able to prevail upon it to plan differently than did the old bureaucratic planning apparatus. Thus, to the last moment, our ideas remained merely theoretical constructs, and the planning apparatus did everything it could to prevent the introduction of new planning methods. Today the planning apparatus is the most powerful enemy of change in the method of planning; it is no longer satisfied with contracts between the center and the enterprises; it is already demanding that next year compulsory targets and tasks be reintroduced.[10]

(4) *Finally, to point four, i.e., the political environment.* As has been already emphasized, in the absence of certain political prerequisites one could not even think of implementing all the planned economic reforms and changes.

First and foremost, one should stress the vital importance of the external political sovereignty of the state, which is the prerequisite of successful economic reforms.

We believed at the time that Czechoslovakia had regained its sovereignty but, unfortunately, this proved to be an error. In spite of official assertions to the contrary, Czechoslovakia does not possess sovereignty today. Consequently, in the prevailing foreign-political situation, one simply cannot vent ideas on fundamental economic and political reforms. They would be rejected both for political and for primitive ideological reasons, since so-called normalization could only be achieved by giving up the idea of fundamental economic reforms. This is the reason for the current and increasingly frequent attacks on the economic reformers, who are accused of being responsible for today's difficulties. As a case in point, our politicians go so far as to reproach me personally for having caused inflation, having ordered the shutdown of unprofitable coal mines and farms, etc.—making me thus responsible for today's lines in front of the food stores.[11]

One further political prerequisite for consistent economic reform is a measure of democratization that breaks down the monopolistic power of the state, and especially of the party bureaucracy. The bureaucracy is in fact the greatest enemy of all economic reforms in the socialist countries. Reforms are contrary to the bureaucrats' interests, so that, without breaking down the power of bureaucracy, it is useless even to think about reforms.[12] This power is supported by a highly centralized, monopolistic political system centered on the power not only of a single political party but, within this party, on a small group of supreme leaders usually found in the Presidium of the Central Committee. The necessary consequence is that the party must be democratized internally, and the monopolistic position of the party must be overcome. By the same token, a degree of democratization must be achieved that would really overcome the supreme power of the bureaucracy. Naturally, at present all this is quite out of the question.

Czechoslovakia must be sovereign both in foreign political and foreign-trade policy. Without changing the structure and composition of foreign trade the economy cannot become efficient. The present composition of foreign trade is responsible for the irrepressible and continually accelerating inflation. It is considered a great advantage for Czechoslovakia that we are able to export such immense quantities of heavy industrial products to socialist markets, mainly to the Soviet Union. In reality, however, this is fatal for the Czechoslovak economy, for we are quite unable to improve the living standards of our people if heavy industry continues to account for such a large proportion of our total output. We are simply unable to procure the necessary consumer goods, services, etc., in return for the products we supply, and structural changes are impossible if this characteristic of foreign trade is maintained.

Our greatest problem today is the construction industry, when it comes to satisfying housing demand. Two years ago Czechoslovakia was second to last in Europe so far as per capita housing construction is concerned, with only Portugal behind us; today, for all I know, we may have moved down to the end of the line, because the construction industry has fallen far short of its targets in recent years. But structural change in this respect is unthinkable at present, for—in spite of the state's control over all resources—the construction industry cannot be expanded without at the same time de-emphasizing heavy industry (relatively, and perhaps even absolutely). Of course, not only the construction industry proper needs improvement, but all industries connected with it, and we are unable to expand all these branches without diverting labor, building materials, imported raw materials, capital, etc., away from the heavy industries. This is impossible, not only because of the pressure to export, but also because of the old planning system which tends to perpetuate the old structure. Finally, heavy industry plays a significant political role in the country; it has the largest number of representatives in all important political bodies and simply will not allow other branches to be given preferential treatment at its own expense.

IV

We were unable to carry out the reforms without the assistance of a democratically selected number of able men in the central organs—in the government, and in the political leadership generally. But under the existing monopolistic political system it is impossible to bring qualified personalities to the top. It is a system in which, automatically, only average and below-average people are vested with important political functions. With mediocrities in top-level positions, it is however impossible to assure effective economic development.

Thus, as long as the old political system is maintained, the most suitable and qualified men will not be made managers of enterprises; managers will continue to be chosen by political criteria—nay, not even by political criteria—but by personal-power criteria used by individual politicians, party secretaries, etc. The politicians select as managers those who would best serve their personal interests, who would support their political position, etc. It was in order to break up this system that we adopted the principle of self-management, that is, the idea of creating workers' councils. It should be pointed out that the transition to self-management in the enterprises was also intended as a means to de-bureaucratize management. We did not plan to place bureaucrats into management, but men and women elected by the staff itself, persons with superior technological knowledge and skill, economic experts who at the same time enjoyed the confidence of their co-workers.

As you know, self-management has been ruled out since 1968, and an extensive propaganda campaign has been launched precisely against this principle. Where new enterprise directors were selected by the worker's councils, as in the Skoda Works at Pilsen, they have since been replaced.

All these unimplemented political conditions lead me to the conclusion that economic reforms cannot be realized in the foreseeable future, which is very unfortunate for the entire economic development of Czechoslovakia. On the other hand, I have to end my evaluation with the very general hope that a fundamental principle of Marxism remains correct, according to which it is economic laws that are decisive in the long run. Although they may be ignored by a political authority, and thus cannot make themselves felt in the economy except through increasing contradictions, these ever more serious economic contradictions will one day have to end in the removal of reactionary and obstructive political authority. Of course, in the long run, this applies not only to Czechoslovakia but also to other socialist states, particularly the Soviet Union. A progressive political authority will eventually emerge and undertake reforms of the socialist economy and the entire society, and these reforms will be quite similar in goals and ideas to those the Czechoslovak reformers had in mind. The old reformers will be vindicated in the end. Of this I am deeply convinced.

Notes

1. *Inter alia,* in my most recent book, *Fakten ueber die tschechoslowakische Wirtschaft (Facts on the Czechoslovak Economy)* (Vienna: Molden, 1969), and in my article "The Economic Impact of Stalinism," *Problems of Communism*, May-June, 1971.

2. The stress of heavy industry is also evident from data in K. Kaplan, *50 let sotsialisma* (50 years of Socialism) (Prague: Svoboda, 1968), especially p. 123 ff., and from *Analysis of Economic Development and Prices in 1968* (unpublished), prepared by a government commission responsible to the author, p. 42 (hereafter abbreviated as *Analysis*).

3. Cf. my *Plan and Market under Socialism* (Prague: Academia, 1967), p. 67.

4. Cf. *Analysis* and *UN Economic Bulletin for Europe*, vol. 18, no. 1. (Geneva, 1966).

5. The Central Committee adopted the pertinent reform resolution, "Main Directions for the Improvement of the Planning and Management of the National Economy" in 1965 (see *Rude Pravo*, Jan. 30, 1965).

6. For some specific information on the matter consult my *Facts on the Czechoslovak Economy*, to appear soon in English as *Czechoslovakia, The Bureaucratic Economy* (New York: International Arts & Sciences Press).

7. *Analysis*, p. 95.

8. The country's export trade, which was directed primarily to the West until 1948, changed drastically, and in 1953 the communist states received close to 80 percent of Czechoslovak exports (*Analysis*, p. 55).

9. As Alexander Dubcek put it: "Democratization of economic administration is an inseparable part of the democratic life of society" (*Bratislava Radio*, Feb. 22, 1968).

10. Cf. the declarations by the Minister of Federal Planning, in *Hospodarska Noviny*, Nov. 28, 1969.

11. Cf., for example, *Rude Pravo*, Oct. 15, 1969 and Jan. 5, Feb. 2, 1970. A good example is the decision of the Central Committee Plenum on "Lessons From the Crisis of Party and Society After the 23rd Party Congress," *Rude Pravo*, Jan. 14, 1971. In his report to the 24th Congress in May 1971, party chief Gustav Husak repeated: "In the economic field, the party leadership ceased directing the development of the national economy and permitted the initiative to be taken by various rightist adventurers, such as Sik, who, at variance with the vital interests of the working people, opened the way to uncontrolled petty-bourgeois activity, to the transformation of public ownership into group ownership, to eliminating the planned management of the national economy, to unrestrained operation of the market, and thus made it impossible for the party and the state to influence the management and development of the national economy. . . . This road would have led to the liquidation of socialist production relations" (*Information Bulletin*, nos. 12-13, 1971, p. 20).

12. Cf. the "Action Program" of the Czechoslovak party in *Rude Pravo*, April 10, 1968.

5

Hungary: Marching Forward

Willy Linder

General Outline

The Hungarian reforms that became an official topic of discussion in the early 1960s and began to be put into effect in 1968 are dominated by two "strategic" considerations:

—greater correlation between enterprise performance and the market, which means considering the market as a yardstick in economic planning, and
—greater decentralization of managerial decision-making.

The lines of action resulting from these two basic considerations are, of course, interdependent, because a greater correlation between the market and economic performance or industrial production is usually possible only when the enterprises participating in this production are given decision alternatives allowing them to adjust to market demand. The individual enterprise's approach to decentralization expresses itself, generally speaking, in a demand for greater autonomy in decision-making.[1] In order to exercise this autonomy properly, however, the individual enterprise must be equipped with the managerial tools that would enable it to receive, interpret, and translate into economic action the various market signals (first and foremost those relating to price policy).

If this demand is to be taken seriously, the enterprise must have the freedom of movement permitting it to adjust autonomously to market developments. The restoration of enterprise decision-making autonomy must be accompanied by a corresponding separation of the enterprise from the central plan; this is simply a reflection of the decentralization of economic decision-making powers. In practice this must occur by either abandoning or considerably reducing the number of indicators (prescribed targets). In Hungary, the transfer of decision-making powers away from the center began with the new reform phase in January 1968, which—after similar reforms had been halted in Czechoslovakia—undoubtedly placed Hungary ahead of all

79

East European states so far as degree of decentralization is concerned.[2] This applies to the areas of production, material-technical supply, foreign trade, investments, prices, finance, the labor market, etc.

The basic structure of a so-called socialist market economy, leaving aside the question of ownership, consists in its search for an optimum mix between binding instructions and autonomy of the individual enterprises; however, the question as to what goals the optimum should be related has not yet been clarified. Undoubtedly the optimum does not relate to growth alone, but to growth within the framework of a more comprehensive socio-political scale of objectives.[3] This scale is determined by political decisions and may therefore be altered in the course of time. Moreover, optimum growth is said to exist only within the limiting qualification of *total equilibrium*,[4] the equilibrium criteria being—as in the West—price stability, balance of payments equilibrium, and full employment. The quest for equilibrium at any price, influenced partially by the reform concepts, has made room for a differentiated growth policy. The postulate of equilibrium determines in the final analysis the rhythm of reforms, a fact that has been given little attention in scholarly literature. And it is the alleged need for equilibrium that is used to justify the fact that the government retains the option to intervene administratively, insofar as this power is an element of the transitional period and not the final result of the reform.[5]

This quest for equilibrium is particularly evident in Hungary, because as decentralization progresses, the system becomes permeated by "elasticities," thereby becoming more flexible but at the same time more unstable, so that a policy of maintaining equilibrium increases in importance as time goes on. However, after consulting the relevant sources and discussing the matter with leading reformers, one has the impression that no clear and definite idea has yet emerged as to how and in what measure priorities (determined by the market) are to be corrected directly by administrative orders ("compulsory indicators"), or more indirectly by state intervention options ("formulae").[6] One can only say that the current mixture of state directives, indirect intervention, and autonomous decision-making by the enterprises cannot yet be considered as the definitive model. Even the reformers themselves are unable to say what this model will look like eventually.

What is clear, however, is that Hungary finds itself in a transitional phase of its economic reform that is to last for 10 to 15 years. The plausible explanation that Budapest gives for this long-term goal and the need—in the meantime—for centrally prescribed indicators is that partial disequilibria can only be removed with the help of structural measures within the framework of a gradual plan. Moreover, political and ideological motives also play a role, and time must pass before the distribution system of a market economy—which is a necessary result of decentralization and which was ideologically banned for so long—becomes politically palatable. Thus, the reformers must fight not only against economic difficulties but are also confronted with the task of eliminating ideological legacies—which gives rise to problems of a political and tactical nature. The Czechoslovak example of 1968 shows that neglecting this point may have tragic consequences. Hungary had its own bitter political experience in 1956, which understandably counsels today's reformers to proceed cautiously.

On the other hand it is quite evident, even today, that Hungary has already gone quite far with the dismantling of central planning, even during the first phase of its reform (1968-70). The central plan as an integral steering element of enterprise operations that predetermines general economic and especially enterprise behavior no longer exists in Hungary in the strict sense. The plan's normative character has been eliminated in broad areas, so that one is justified, in the case of Hungary—using the criteria formulated by Professor Karl C. Thalheim[7]—in speaking of the beginnings of a real system-change as distinguished from a "within-system change," i.e., a mere change in procedures. This development is most apparent in the areas of production, foreign trade, investment, and price policy.

Production

The first signs of adjustment to the new trend were apparent in over-all production policy. In 1968, that is, in the first year of the reform, twenty percent of the total volume of output was still centrally decreed. This was to be reduced to twelve percent by the end of 1969, and it is not to exceed ten percent by the end of the first reform phase (end of 1970). Compulsory production amounts primarily to the state's delivery commitments abroad, and from the state's own requirements (for social services, military needs, major structure-determining categories of goods, etc.), that is, the state's requirements for capital goods in order to fulfill its investment plans.[8]

Thus, the Hungarian enterprises have gained a very respectable degree of decision-making autonomy in the production field. The question, of course, arises as to whether they will actually be able to take advantage of this autonomy, or whether they will be prevented from doing so by existing restrictions in other fields. Insofar as the inputs of the single production units are concerned, some of the requisite raw materials could be bought freely; in certain sectors where shortages exist, controls would be maintained during the transitional period; state controls will naturally remain in force chiefly for imported raw materials[9] and for materials whose supply might fall short of potential demand (equilibrium requirement!). These last include sulphur, certain types of steel, Diesel engines, certain cables, newsprint, imported coal, etc. The list is to be gradually reduced. In any case, the principle of direct allocation has been given up as a determinant of the system.

Trade

The principle that trade in capital goods is to be guided by market requirements was accepted as a long-term goal. As is the case with consumer goods, enterprises may relinquish traditional trade channels and organize new marketing patterns better suited to the distribution of their particular output.

Naturally, the administrative setting of production deadlines also had to be abolished (delivery dates are to be determined by the contracting parties). As a result—to put it simply—purchase and sale are now integrated into the relaxed structure of over-all production policy. Administrative intervention is still a possibility, if required to correct or to avoid disequilibria.

It is quite likely that an overly hasty and drastic release of foreign trade from administrative control may cause pressure resulting from domestic shortages that would affect imports to an unbearable degree.[10] Therefore, foreign trade restrictions and the instruments of direct state intervention have been retained; e.g., foreign exchange controls, quotas, foreign trade permits, and import deposits. The spirit in which interventions in foreign trade are made will be decisive: they could be used either as protective measures pure and simple, favoring those sectors of the domestic economy that are not sufficiently competitive internationally, or they could be justified by the need for equilibrium and used as a means to stimulate domestic efficiency by increasing the pressure of foreign competition.[11] From first-hand experience, one gathers the impression that Hungarian foreign trade policy is very definitely departing from its former, strictly bilateral patterns and is becoming more flexible, more alert to comparative cost advantages. It would surely be premature to say that Hungary has already opted for a multilateral system of trade; this is impossible for the time being because Hungary, like all the other Soviet-bloc countries, is integrated within the Comecon foreign trade system. About eighty percent of Hungary's industrial output is exported to socialist countries, and about sixty-six percent of Hungary's raw materials are imported from the bloc. Moreover, the question of convertibility of the forint, which is an indispensable precondition for enterprise freedom in foreign trade, remains purely academic.

Foreign trade seems therefore to be substantially determined by historically-developed foreign trade structures,[12] as well as by the continuation of strict foreign exchange controls and the system of multiple exchange rates (the import rouble still returns much less than the import dollar).[13] This situation cannot, however, conceal the fact that Hungary is experiencing not only a change in its foreign trade philosophy, but is also making progress toward relaxing formerly rigid trade policy maxims. This is of vital importance for the country, because over forty percent of its national income derives from foreign trade; Hungary satisfies fifty percent of its raw material needs via imports; and the one percent average annual increase in national income over the past five years was accompanied by a two percent rise in imports.[14] Thus, Hungary is very dependent on foreign trade, and for this reason the reformers are intensely occupied with foreign trade problems.[15] Only the future will tell what model of foreign trade will eventually emerge from the current reforms.

Investment

Practically all reform models currently discussed or being implemented in Eastern Europe indicate that, apart from the problems of price policy, the greatest difficulties are encountered in decentralizing managerial decision-making in the field of investment. This is not at all astonishing, because in the orthodox thinking of a planned economy the investment plan represents the crux of the planning concept in general; it is investment policy that determines the direction of economic development, and investment control has proved to be one of the most important tools in directing the operations of the individual enterprise. Moreover, the decentralization of managerial decision-making in the field of investment eventually becomes an obstacle to all those reform models that, although "rationalized," retain a relatively dense network of centrally prescribed and binding indicators. Consequently, we see two investment cycles emerge: a centrally planned cycle, and one resulting from individualized investment decisions; the latter, although predictable to a certain degree, is not subject any more to planning in the proper sense. This leads however to new planning problems that become all-embracing (due to the interdependence among the various sectors of the economy). There is hardly any other field in which the reformers are faced by a greater dilemma resulting from economic interdependence than in investment policy. This is the main reason why, for example, the Kosygin reform has thus far failed even to approach its originally announced goal of investment decentralization.[16] The degree of decentralization of investment decisions may be regarded as a main indication, as a test case, of the existing will to reform, of the drive and "muscle" behind the reform blueprint; but it is also of decisive economic relevance, because the managerial autonomy of the individual enterprise in investment decisions will be judged according to the enterprise's ability to find its optimum size from the standpoint of the market. It may be safely assumed that the old investment policy did much to promote the development of enterprises smaller than the economic optimum.[17]

The situation in Hungary looks as follows: a distinction is made between two categories of investment: namely, state (or government) investment (decision-making being vested with the respective ministries of government), and investment determined autonomously by the enterprises. State investments comprise major individual projects as well as group investments, all of them designed to realize a common state-determined investment objective. By nature they are considered true development investments (affecting power, transportation, and the like). While the state initiates group investments, most of them are carried out on a decentralized basis. Centralized investments are supposed to affect infrastructural projects only.

Decentralized investments include all those categories in which individual enterprises can adapt to the market. In this context, it is interesting to find that the risk of such investments is looked upon as pure entrepreneurial risk, as part of "managerial risk" in general. This change in attitude signifies a clear departure from the old investment philosophy and the adoption of a true enterpreneurial—one is almost tempted to say capitalistic—attitude. This "detail" has a certain symbolic significance. In Budapest one points to it as an important argument to the effect that the Hungarian variety of economic reform is not meant to be a sub-species of workers' self-management.

Some relevant facts should suffice to evaluate this model of decision-making in the field of investments. According to information obtained in Budapest decentralized investment in 1970 approached fifty percent of total investment; a figure that compares more than favorably with all other reform concepts. This percentage is to be increased to 57 by 1975. The final proportion between centralization and decentralization in the investment sector is hardly predictable because of the absence of a theoretical model of decision-making that could solve the question of optimum efficiency in investments.[18]

A further item must be considered within the framework of investment policy, namely the *financing of investments*. Obviously the authority of individual enterprises to determine their own investments depends largely on the availability of funds. Recent figures show that about fifty percent of all (long-term) investments are still financed by the state budget, thirteen to fifteen percent by bank loans, and thirty-five to thirty-seven percent by the enterprises' own resources (one-half of the short-term financing is done by means of bank loans, and all variable capital is financed either internally or by bank credit).[19] Such resources are now available because the old system of profit deductions in favor of the state was replaced by a new system of profit taxation. It remains to be seen how successful this new method of enhancing the role of enterprise self-financing will be.

It is mainly in the area of credit policy that government influence is, as expected, relatively strong even today. This influence is exercised mainly in the granting and repayment of credit and, to a certain extent, in taxation policy (through which the government can exert a direct influence on the self-financing ability of the enterprises). This leverage exists because of the absence of competition in the credit sector, that is, because the monopolization of credit by the state can directly influence the behavior of the enterprises. As a result, there is the danger of erroneous investment, mainly because of the application of differentiated interest rates by the state.

On the other hand it is, of course, also true that, if the price structure is distorted, the danger of such misdirected investment could not be excluded even if "neutral," non-discriminatory, credit rates were applied. It is not convincing to argue that the differentiated application of credit policy might in some way neutralize the discriminating effects of a distorted price structure. In any case, a non-discriminatory credit policy requires market-oriented prices—in other words, a price reform.

The Hungarian reformers are aware of these problems. They are also aware that the return to a more flexible credit policy is only the first step toward a much more far-reaching remonetization of the economy,[20] and that the full benefits of bringing the market into the system could be reaped only if the socialist economy adopts an active monetary policy. Consequently, the old thesis that the economy must be "controlled by the rouble" (or the forint) must be discarded. When enterprises may accumulate investment funds of their own, it is necessary to establish a capital-market institution that would not only provide the enterprises with investment opportunities but would also see to it that idle investment funds were free to circulate and seek their most productive use. This would give money, which today has a mainly static, accounting role its real function of allocating resources, thus exposing the credit sector to the influence of competition. It is clear that a capital market under socialism could never assume the form it takes under capitalism, if only because of the difference in property relations between the two systems. However, the main objective here is to bring back money as an active economic entity. These problems are being discussed in the "inner circles" of the Hungarian reformers, and practical results may be expected during the second phase of the reform.

The balance sheet shows that Hungarian investment policy still has many centralistically-motivated restrictions, some of which are symptoms of the transitional period and others are inherent in the system. On the other hand, one must say that Hungary, after only a couple of years of reform, has taken decentralization to a stage that, considering the limited field of maneuver allowed in Eastern Europe, must be viewed as innovative. Considering also the will of the Hungarian reformers to continue along this new path, the political climate permitting, Hungary is obviously very progressive in the matter of economic reform.

Price Policy

Price policy is a further and highly important area of reform, and Hungary has embarked upon a remarkable course in this respect as well. According to the most authoritative expert in this field, Professor Csikos-Nagy, the general objective is to let prices function, as in the pre-communist past, as market signals and, at the same time, to implement a structural reform establishing a more appropriate relationship between the excessively low prices of services and certain consumer goods and the excessively high prices of consumer durables. This means that prices are increasingly reflecting the structure of costs; in Csikos' words, they are to reflect production policy inputs. A further objective is to reduce the large gap between wholesale and retail prices—to create a price system that is no longer based on a dualistic but on a uniform market-oriented concept of value.[21] These problems are related to the need for reorganizing the clearly hypertrophic subsidy system, a system under which eighty percent of the turnover tax revenue had to be used to finance the gap between input costs and output prices. By threatening to withdraw subsidies, the government has an effective means of pushing the enterprises toward the market. As a prerequisite, however, the enterprises must, of course, be allowed some room for maneuver in their price policy. A reform of the turnover tax is also a must; the tax was, in fact, modified at the very beginning of the first reform phase but continues to be a problem. Further tax reforms are planned that are to make the turnover tax non-discriminatory.[22]

Price reforms are known to be among the most thorny tasks for the reformers, because they involve not only economic problems but political and social ones as well. For this reason, price reforms must proceed smoothly and be carried out with subtlety. Above all they should proceed in harmony with other structure-improving measures, because an excessively abrupt relaxation of price policy would cause wide price fluctuations, particularly in markets suffering from major disequilibrium. Such fluctuations can be avoided only by adjusting the production capacities of enterprises in the branches suffering disequilibria, that is, by structural measures that cannot be carried out overnight. Consequently, price reforms are to be attained by means of a four-tier price system consisting of centrally fixed prices, maximum prices, "limit" prices (allowed to fluctuate between official limits), and free prices. Greater importance is to be attached to free prices as the transitional period progresses.

The following tables reveal the actual distribution of price groups. This chronological sequence shows that a remarkable transformation has been taking place in the initial years of the reform. Considering that, in the orthodox philosophy of economic planning, the administrative and centralized fixing of prices is a main feature, it is

Relative Share of Price Groups in Total Output

Groups	1968	1969 (percent)	1971
Fixed Prices	20	20	12
Maximum Prices	30	30	38
Limit Prices	27	20	–
Free Prices	23	30	50
	100	100	100

Relative Share of Price Groups in Selected Industries

Industries	Fixed Prices	Maximum Prices	Limit Prices (percent)	Free Prices	Total
Raw materials and typical semi-finished goods	30	40	2	28	100
Processing Industry	1	10	4	85	100
Agriculture	60	10[a]	20[b]	10	100
Consumer goods (state trading and free market)	20	30	27	23	100

[a]Allowed to fluctuate within strict officially prescribed margins.
[b]Allowed to fluctuate within more liberal officially prescribed margins.
Source: R. Nyers in *Hospodarske Noviny*, July 25, 1969

impressive to note, that as early as 1968 only twenty percent of the total output (most fuels and building materials and thirty percent of the foodstuffs) was sold at fixed prices.[23] Moreover, once prices have been freed from controls, the price authorities are bound to interfere no longer. An "early warning system" offers opportunities for price corrections in the event of clear market abuse, which may occur because some branches of industry are so heavily concentrated that competition can no longer function as a reliable price-determining factor. But even in such cases the price authorities may not intervene on their own initiative. It is rumored in Budapest that the price-controlling authority will not survive for long.

Of course, even a price reform cannot yield the full benefit of the market-oriented economy envisaged by Hungarian reformers so long as a system of multiple exchange rates persists in foreign trade. Only after a nondiscriminatory, competitive exchange-rate system has been established will it be possible for the domestic price level to adjust to the international price level, and for Hungarian industries to have a genuine yardstick by which to measure their international competitiveness.

Conclusion

In early 1968, Hungary embarked upon and by now has already partially implemented a far-reaching decentralization concept unequalled by any of the other socialist states of the Soviet bloc since Czechoslovakia undertook its abortive reform experiment.

The record of Hungary's progress would be equally clear if we extended our analysis of production, trade, investment, and price policy to wage and personnel policy as well. To be sure, a formula for government intervention does indeed continue to exist and still exceeds by far what a conventional market economy might tolerate. But even in this respect a number of modifications may be made in the course of the reform period.

One difficult problem in the case of Hungary is that the selection of enterprise managers still rests with the central ministries. Professor Ota Sik has repeatedly emphasized that reforms can succeed only if the enterprises are made entirely autonomous in their personnel policies. Only an insider can judge whether this requirement is equally imperative for Hungary. Perhaps the fact that in Hungary one constantly encounters skepticism as to the *raison d'être* of industrial ministries suggests that the reform will lead to some changes in this field as well. Indeed, the continued existence of such ministries becomes more questionable as decentralization progresses.

At the close of 1971, there are complaints that investment plans continue to be over-ambitious as compared to available capacity (non-completed projects accounted for about eighty percent of the value of total investment funds in 1971); this leads to inflationary pressures and to greater enterprise indebtedness. The labor shortage is another perennial problem—intensified perhaps by growing turn-over and slackening labor discipline—adversely affecting enterprise planning and efficiency. In a general sense, these domestic difficulties are reflected in foreign trade, where the growing influx of capital and consumer goods from the West and the general unattractiveness of Hungarian exports to the West have been burdening the balance of trade quite seriously. All this prompted Premier Fock to announce temporary curbs on investments and imports.[24]

In spite of these shortcomings, however, most of which have been plaguing the Hungarian economy for a long time, there are no indications of a retreat from the principles of the new economic mechanism—only occasional reversals and a pace slower than envisaged for the full implementation of these principles. The important thing is that central planning of the command type has changed not merely in detail but in principle, and that the enterprises have been given decision-making autonomy, which is quite different from the illusion of enterprise freedom prevailing in other socialist countries.

Notes

1. On the problem in general, see A. Thomas Marschak, "Centralized versus Decentralized Resource Allocation," *The Quarterly Journal of Economics*, vol. 9, no. 4, November 1968.

2. The 1968 reform was preceded by intensive discussion; see, for example, Ernst Schmidt-Papp, "Die oekonomische Reformbewegung in Ungarn und der neue Wirtschaftsmechanismus" (The Economic Reform Movement in Hungary and the New Economic Mechanism), in K.C. Thalheim and H.H. Hoehmann, eds., *Wirtschaftsreformen in Osteuropa* (Economic Reforms in East Europe) (Cologne, 1968), p. 188 ff.

3. "Every important economic reform is, at the same time, a social and political reform as well, according to Jozsef Bognar, "Economic Reform and International Economic Policy," *The New Hungarian Quarterly*, vol. 9, no. 32, Winter 1968, p. 80; also Rezso Nyers, "Social and Political Effects of the New Economic Mechanism," *The New Hungarian Quarterly*, vol. 10, no. 34, Summer 1969, p. 3 ff.

4. According to Jozsef Bognar, *Les nouveaux mecanismes de l'économie socialiste en Hongrie* (The New Mechanisms of the Socialist Economy in Hungary) (Paris, 1969), p. 104: "Réforme n'est pas synonyme de révolution, ce qui revient à dire que les changements de situation . . . doivent se réaliser dans des conditions d'équilibre relatif, ou plus exactement, dans une situation de déséquilibre tolérable" (Reform is not identical with revolution. In other words, changes . . . have to be effected under conditions of relative equilibrium or, more exactly, under conditions of tolerable disequilibrium). See also Imre Vajda, "Gesamtwirtschaftliche Planung und die Rolle der Unternehmung in der sozialistischen Wirtschaft Ungarns (Macro-economic Planning and the Role of Enterprises in the Hungarian Socialist Economy)," *Osteuropa-Wirtschaft*, no. 2, 1967, p. 108 ff. Deputy Prime Minister Peter Valyi in "Planned Economy and Financial Policy," *The New Hungarian Quarterly*, vol. 9, 1968, p. 64 states: "Every economic programme has two cornerstones around which the partial problems involved in the solution are grouped. These are economic growth and economic equilibrium."

5. Cf. O. Gado, "The New System of Trade in Production Goods," *Reform of the Economic Mechanism in Hungary* (Budapest, 1969), p. 111.

6. I. Friss, "Principal Features of the New System of Planning, Economic Control, and Management in Hungary," in Gado, op. cit., p. 12. Also, Jozsef Bognar, "Wirtschaftsreform und Ost-West Handel (Economic Reform and East-West Trade)," *Studienhandbuch der Ungarischen Wirtschaft, Politik und Kultur* (Budapest, 1968), vol. 3, p. 33. According to Attila Madarasi, "Centralization and Decentralization in Investment Decisions," (paper presented at the CESES Meeting, Sept. 3-5, 1969, p. 5): "The problem of decentralization

never emerges as an end in itself, but always reflects the particular circumstances and relations as well as the given level of development, and all this with the view to concrete economic targets. Therefore, the adopted arrangements are always of relative character and have to be handled in an elastic way. The art of economic management consists in finding the optimum proportion of centralization and decentralization in the actual situation."

7. Karl C. Thalheim, "Deuten die Wirtschaftsreformen in den Ostblocklaendern auf einen Systemwandel?" (Do the East European Economic Reforms Betoken a Change of System?), *Osteuropa-Wirtschaft*, Stuttgart, 1965, no. 4, p. 311 ff.

8. In the future, enterprises will have the right to participate in the conclusion of international agreements. (Cf. Julius Nagy's article in *Osteuropa-Wirtschaft*, no. 3, 1968, p. 225 ff.)

9. Cf. Gado, op. cit., p. 131.

10. "The new system is based on the autonomy of the productive enterprises in respect to both production and sales. The enterprises are free to establish their production programs, to procure the materials necessary for their production, and to sell their own output. Such an interpretation of enterprise autonomy assumes and necessitates direct relations between producers and buyers—their freedom to contract." (Ibid., p. 112.)

11. About one-third of the long-term contracts are assigned by comprehensive bidding (cf. J. Balint, "Some Problems of the Implementation of Economic Reforms," *Kozgazdasagi Szemle*, July-August 1969, p. 787).

12. Cf. Theodor Zotschew, "Wirtschaftliche Entwicklung und gegenseitige Handelsbeziehungen der suedosteuropaeischen Staaten" (Economic Development and Trade Relations Among the Southeast European States), *Wirtschaftswissenchaftliche Suedosteuropa-Forschung, Festschrift fuer Professor Hermann Gross* (Economic Research on Southeast Europe, Undertaken in Honor of Professor Hermann Gross) (Munich, 1963), p. 35 ff.

13. Cf. Jozsef Bognar, op. cit., p. 36.

14. Ibid., p. 35.

15. Cf. Imre Vajda, *The Role of Foreign Trade in a Socialist Economy* (Budapest, 1965); also Werner Gumpel, "Ungarn" (Hungary), in W. Gumpel and H. Vogel, eds., *Gegenwartsfragen der Ost-Wirtschaft* (Contemporary Problems of the Eastern Economies) (Munich and Vienna, 1968), vol. 5, p. 38 ff.

16. Cf. Keith Bush, "The Implementation of the Soviet Economic Reform," paper presented to the CESES Meeting, 1969.

17. Cf. Walter Wittmann, "Einige Aspekte der Investitionsfor-

cierung der Oststaaten" (Some Aspects of Forced Investments in Eastern Europe), in *Wirtschaftfragen in und zwischen Ost und West* (Economic Problems in and between East and West) (Duesseldorf and Vienna, 1966).

18. Cf. J. Tinbergen, "Die Tendenzen im oekonomischen Denken Ost-Europas (Tendencies in East European Economic Thought)," lecture at the University of Zurich, November 25, 1968.

19. Cf. Deputy Prime Minister Matyas Timar, "Conditions of Economic Growth under the New Mechanism," *Kozgazdasagi Szemle*, December 1968, pp. 1397-99; and J. Saro, "The Experience of Planning Variable Costs," *Penzugyi Szemle*, July 1969, p. 584.

20. Cf. Egon Kemenes, "Von der Geldwirtschaft zur Geldpolitik—zwanzig Jahre ungarische Finanzen (From Monetary Economy to Monetary Policy—Twenty Years of Hungarian Finance)," *Studienhandbuch der ungarischen Wirtschaft, Politik und Kultur* (Handbook of the Hungarian Economy, Politics, and Culture) (Budapest, 1968), vol. III, p. 42 ff., and Gregory Grossman, "The Reforms and Money," paper presented to the CESES Meeting, 1969, p. 113 ff.

21. Cf. B. Csikos-Nagy, "The New Hungarian Price System," in Gado, op. cit., p. 113 ff.

22. Ibid., p. 155 ff.

23. It is interesting to note that the planners treat flexible prices as a function of their share in total prices and of the change in government-directed prices. Cf. Sp. Kopatsky, "Industrial Producer Forces and Profits," *Kozgazdasagi Szemle*, June 1968.

24. See the proceedings of an economic conference in October 1971, highlighted by Fock's speech in *Nepszabadsag*, Oct. 23 and 24, 1971. They confirm previous assessments, e.g., by J. Bognar, "Two Years of the Hungarian New Economic Mechanism," *Kozgazdasagi Szemle*, January 1970.

Poland: On Again — Off Again

Michael Gamarnikow

I

Poland's experience with economic reforms has been rather traumatic and hardly encouraging. The record shows that, since 1957, the Polish regime has made three abortive attempts to implement three qualitatively different blueprints of a new system of planning and management. Each time, however, the reform program in question had to be abandoned, either because of the strong opposition of dogmatic elements in the party establishment and the effectiveness of subtle sabotage employed by entrenched bureaucrats in the economic apparatus, or under the pressure of an acute economic crisis.

The main reason for this dismal record is that the Polish ruling elite has acquired the habit of treating economic reforms as a convenient political football in its perennial factional infighting. The blame for this must be shared equally by the various types of hardliner, by the technocrats, by the middle-of-the-roaders, and by the quasi-liberals. The net effect is that, unlike Hungary, for instance, there are very few party politicians in Poland who can claim to have taken a consistent positive stand on the issue of the new economic model. Here, Gomulka himself was, of course, the principal culprit. It was his ambivalent and often opportunistic style of leadership that was primarily responsible for the fact that Poland, once the outstanding pioneer in the field of economic reforms, must now be counted among the most persistent footdraggers.

But neither the lack of a coherent policy line nor the absence of a firm and consistent leadership can absolve the Polish ruling elite from sharing a large part of responsibility for Poland's "on again–off again" approach to the essential problem of new methods of planning and management. After all, it was not Gomulka, but the other top members of the establishment who quite deliberately decided to treat economic reforms as a legitimate, though more often than not, side issue in their periodic power struggles.

II

The first and the most comprehensive version of the Polish economic model, as evolved during the early post-October 1956 period, never had much of a chance of progressing beyond the stage of a coherent theoretical blueprint. This first version could be summarized as follows:[1]

The economy was to be decentralized quite drastically by dismantling the bureaucratic superstructure and giving considerable autonomy to the individual enterprise, which should be self-supporting and strive for the highest degree of profitability. Moreover, market forces should be taken increasingly into account, as the enterprise was to sell its output at prices reflecting the costs of production and supply and demand. Consequently, a general reform of wages and other costs of inputs as well as prices of outputs was considered necessary.

Thus, the Polish model revealed a strong influence of the Yugoslav experience at that time and even went beyond it, because it placed greater reliance on the market, as the noted Oskar Lange made clear.[2]

The main reason for the abortive result of this wide-ranging proposal was that the Polish economic reformers in the 1956-57 period wanted to achieve too much, too soon: The time was not yet ripe for implementing pragmatic reforms on such a scale. The other countries of the Soviet bloc, including some that later introduced economic reforms much along the lines advocated in Poland in the mid-1950s, regarded the 1956-57 blueprint of the Polish economic model as the epitome of ideological revisionism. Indeed, those countries applied strong pressure on the Gomulka regime to "stop playing with fire."[3]

Far more decisive than this hostile outside pressure was, however, the active resistance of the dogmatic forces within the Polish establishment. Those forces, defeated temporarily in October 1956, were fighting against the implementation of the new model both on ideological and on personal grounds, since their vested interests and special privileges would be seriously threatened by the new organizational and operational patterns foreseen in the reform blueprint. But the new economic model, as such, was not the primary target of the hardliners' counter-offensive. What they were really aiming at was to hasten the failure of the new economic model and use that as the political leverage—to restore their power within the party, as it existed prior to the October upheaval. With this objective in mind, the bureaucratic superstructure sabotaged many experiments intended as pilot schemes for the new methods of planning and management.

By late 1959, the dogmatic counter-offensive achieved most of its objectives. The Polish Economic Council—a body of experts created for the express purpose of devising the theoretical principles of the new economic model—had for all practical purposes ceased to exist.[4] The changes already implemented in the organizational structure of Polish industry were effectively countered by the strengthening of centralized control with its inevitable profusion of operational directives. The proposed reform of wages and prices, due to be implemented in 1958, was abandoned altogether. The "Workers Councils," which were originally intended to co-manage independent enterprises, were shorn of their essential prerogatives, granted in the 1956 legislation. At the same time, the concept of a Yugoslav-type workers' self-management system was formally condemned.

More significant still was a remarkable political comeback of unrepentant foes of economic reform. By mid-1959, all those members of the ruling elite genuinely associated with the October program of political and economic reforms had been effectively ousted from positions of authority and, in many cases, cast into political oblivion. This resulted in a very meaningful shift in the balance of power within the party leadership, because three notorious hardliners from the old days were appointed to top economic positions.[5] Shortly afterwards the powers of the central planners were greatly strengthened,[6] and that was—for all practical purposes— the end of the first phase of economic reform in Poland.

III

The return to a monocentric economic system and to the arbitrary methods of direct controls inevitably resulted in serious economic difficulties that reached their climax in the winter of 1962-63. In the fall of 1963, the Polish ruling elite began again to look more critically at arbitrary methods of planning and management. This led to a renewal of interest in the economic reforms that were so hastily abandoned after the dogmatic restoration. Thus, in March 1964, the party leaders, preparing for their Fourth Congress in June, published a set of theses outlining, among other things, certain concrete methods of planning and management intended to reactivate some aspects of the new economic model.[7]

The Congress itself passed a resolution calling for greater decentralization of decision-making, the need to accept profitability and strict cost accounting as "the basic criteria for evaluating economic efficiency," as well as for careful market research. A month later, a lengthy decree attempted to institutionalize these decisions: implement the requested economic effectiveness, strict cost accounting, profitability, and abidance by potential demand. It also requested substituting several variants of the draft plan for the single and mandatory central plan, allowing some leeway before final decisions were made. But the decree added many bureaucratic safeguards, such as a controlling superstructure of about ten central bodies, and it failed to specify what would happen if sound economic consideration clashed with political and ideological tenets. All this tended to neutralize the positive aspects of the reform. A few months later, new methods of investment financing called for greater reliance on repayable and interest-bearing bank loans, except for "priority investments." Yet, in July 1965, it was announced that a "free movement of prices, uncontrolled by the state, or the spontaneous shaping of prices by . . . supply and demand" were inadmissible.[8]

While several proposals of the 1964 theses were subsequently watered down, the bulk of them did survive, and a more or less definite program of economic reforms based on this truncated blueprint was approved by the Central Committee Plenum held in July 1965.[9]

Thus, after an interval of nearly six years, economic pragmatism had again become part of the official policy line in Poland. But the political situation within the party establishment was by then entirely different from what prevailed in the early post-October 1956 period. In 1956, the dogmatic elements within the Polish ruling elite were decisively beaten and were in full political retreat. The quasi-liberal faction, in favor of economic reforms, held the levers of power and—what is equally important—controlled the information media and used them very extensively to promote a more pragmatic concept of "socialism." By contrast, the 1964-65 version of the reform blueprint was devised and sponsored by the middle-of-the-road apparatchiki, not as an article of faith, but under the pressure of economic necessity. Thus, while the protagonists of the 1956-57 version of the Polish economic model were genuinely convinced that the orthodox system of planning and management had outlived any usefulness it ever had, the hesitant promoters of the 1964-65 edition of partial and emasculated economic reforms were not. Besides, they distrusted any structural and institutional changes which could deprive the party establishment of its "leading role" in economic affairs.

This lack of political will to push through meaningful change in the methods of planning and management explains the different approach to the whole issue of economic reforms in the mid-1960s. Unlike the late 1950s, there was far less stress on the theoretical rationale behind the proposed measures and, apart from a few rather academic dissertations on the subject of the profit motive, very little was said about the operational pattern of the new system. All emphasis was put on preparing a number of elaborate bureaucratic measures necessary (so it was argued) to set the new system in motion. But the hodgepodge combination of unrelated half-measures was replete with built-in safety valves clearly intended to perpetuate bureaucratic controls.

Despite all its limitations, the 1964-65 blueprint of economic reforms did contain some long-term potentialities. The proposed changes in the methods of planning and management (however inadequate) were nonetheless a step in the right direction. They could well serve as a starting point for developing a broader and more cohesive program of economic reform, given the political will to put such a program into effect. All that was needed to make those pragmatic measures fully operational was a change of heart on the part of the Polish ruling elite.

So, even this emasculated version of economic reforms was unacceptable to the powerful pressure groups of political hardliners and entrenched bureaucrats. They fought approval of the blueprint every inch of the way, playing rather skillfully on the inborn apprehensions and reservations of Gomulka and his close associates. And when the 1964-65 version of the new economic model had finally become an integral part of the official party program, the dogmatists and hardliners reverted to their favorite tactics of procrastination and other forms of bureaucratic sabotage. These tactics proved so effective that all the proposed reform measures remained essentially on paper. In July 1967, the editor-in-chief of *Zycie Gospodarcze*, press organ of the economic reformers, complained bitterly that although two years have already passed since the final approval of the new methods of planning and management by the Central Committee Plenum, "the actual implementation of the reforms on all levels still left much to be desired."[10]

Discussing the reasons why the 1964-65 version of the new model failed to get off the ground, *Zycie Gospodarcze* put the main blame on the "old habits and conditioned reflexes that are the heritage of the old system." It also castigated the dogmatic mentality of the people entrusted with implementing the new system on the trust and enterprise level: "They stick to old methods and familiar routine—charged the reformist weekly—in the hope that the old ways will return."[11] This was as close to an accusation that the reforms were being sabotaged as the party censors would permit.

But, by the time these facts appeared in print, the dogmatists were already marshalling their forces for a counter-offensive. As usual, however, neither the new economic model nor the economic reformers were their real target. The carefully prepared attacks on the economic reforms and their protagonists were meant only to serve as the means to a far more ambitious bid for supreme political power in Poland. The economic reformers were simply chosen as the initial objective because—among other things—so many of them happened to be of Jewish origin.

Uncomprehensible as this might seem to a Western mind, the event which made Polish economic reformers (and—through guilt by association—their reform program, too) especially vulnerable was of all things the Arab-Israeli war in June 1967. People uninitiated in the ways of party politics in Poland and in the tactics of factional warfare among communist elites would fail to see any logical connection between the defeat of the Arab armies in the Sinai peninsula and the fate of economic reform in far-away Poland. But the Polish hardliners grasped the internal implications of Moscow's pro-Arab policy very quickly indeed.

The net effect was that anti-Semitism became a legitimate political weapon in the intra-party struggle for power. This weapon, used at first against some small fry in the mass communication media, began to be exploited to the utmost after the student revolt of March 1968 had shaken the very foundations of Gomulka's regime. It turned out that the main blame for this outburst of political dissent was authoritatively attributed to a "Zionist plot" directed against People's Poland. This, in turn, made anyone of Jewish origin a candidate for political purge. The dogmatists and hardliners, who had espoused anti-Semitism as a political weapon, became the principal witch-hunters.

Prominent economic reformers, such as Professor Brus, were among the earliest victims. They were publicly denounced not only as "Zionist agents," but also as "the principal carriers of the deadly bacilli of economic revisionism."[12] For the hardliners and their allies were not satisfied with hounding the leading reformers out of their jobs, out of public life, and even out of the country.[13] They had come to the conclusion that the time was ripe to deal a death blow to the very idea of economic reform and thus to destroy, once and for all, the perennial threat to their vested interests.

Their assessment was based on quite valid premises. The middle of 1968 was a very suitable time for such an all-out attack on the new economic model. As a prelude to the invasion of Czechoslovakia, Moscow and its allies had put into high gear an ideological offensive of their own directed against all manifestations of the "revisionist" heresy, and both the Czechoslovak and Yugoslav economic reforms were denounced almost daily in Soviet, East German, and Bulgarian periodicals. In Poland, economic reformers and their supporters in the party establishment were in no position to defend themselves and their pragmatic concepts. The middle-of-the-roaders, on their part, were only too glad to see the criticism of the past-March days deflected to a different target.

This state of affairs offered a unique opportunity to all foes of economic reform to settle their accounts once and for all. To create a proper political atmosphere, various third-rate scholars and theoreticians were mobilized for a massive propaganda campaign that grossly exaggerated the political threat inherent in the reforms. Thus, in one article, the pragmatic reformers were accused of advocating an economic system in which "real power will pass into the hands of a narrow group of economic experts, (while) . . . the leading role of the party would be reduced to a minimum."[14]

This specter of the technocrats exploiting the economic reform program so as to take over the political reins, was, of course, deliberately raised by the hardliners in order to secure the support of the party apparatus in their own drive for power. On the one hand, it was a blatant appeal to vested interests of this special group; on the other, it made quite clear that the real targets of the denunciations were not the hapless reformers (since they were already out, anyway), but those members of the party establishment who had supported the reformers' "revisionist" and "anti-socialist" ideas and provided them with the seal of ideological legitimacy. In this sense, the attacks on economic reforms were merely a reflection of the struggle for political power.

But, while for the foes of Gomulka the economic reforms were only a side issue, or rather a convenient stick with which to beat their political opponents, the third-rate scholars and obscure traditionalist theoreticians had their own private accounts to settle. For more than a decade they had to watch as the reformers basked in international limelight, while their own dogmatic brand of "Marxism" was held in contempt. Now (so they thought) their hour had struck, and they had a chance to take revenge for all the past slights in the field of scholarship and public recognition. They not only denounced the "market mechanism" for promoting "enrichment as the central value of life,"[15] but hurled epithets right and left. The ideas of a prominent Polish reformer, Professor Kurowski, were described as "a very typical example of subversion through vulgar bourgeois thought—supervision that attempted to eliminate the Marxist theory of historical materialism and to undermine the victorious prospects of the socialist system."[16] Other progressive economists in Poland were accused of "working hard to purge our economic theory of all the Marxist 'myths' and 'dogmas,'" of entrenching themselves in "anti-socialist and revisionist positions," and of "acting as apologists for bourgeois ideology."[17]

This campaign of denunciations continued for several months. And the very fact that most of those attacks were published in *Trybuna Ludu*, the central organ of the Polish communist party, gave them the stamp of official authority. The only real weakness of this frontal attack on the theory and practice of economic reform was the obvious unwillingness of reputable economists and political theoreticians to participate in such public contumely. Slowly but inexorably the anti-reform campaign in Poland began to lose momentum.

This gave the serious middle-of-the-road economists a chance to defend at least the vestiges of a pragmatic approach to economic problems. A typical example was the article written by M. Mieszczan-kowski in June 1968.[18] The author paid lip service to the party line by condemning "revisionism" in economic thinking (although in very restrained terms). But the main thrust of his article was directed against "leftist revisionists," whom he sharply criticized for their attempts "to eliminate or to restrict such useful tools of economic analysis as the law of value, the profit motive, material incentives, or cost accounting methods." Moreover, the author made it understood (between the lines) that those "leftist revisionists" whom he accused of "spreading the cheap slogans of political and social demagogy" and of propagating economic solutions "devoid of any scientific foundations and practical usefulness"[19] were, in fact, the notorious ultra-dogmatists whose articles appeared so prominently in *Trybuna Ludu* only a few months ago.

Under the impact of articles such as Mieszczankowski's, the virulent campaign against all forms of economic reform lost much of its initial momentum. The attacks against "economic revisionism" were briefly revived after the invasion of Czechoslovakia, when a substantial number of clearly mandatory articles against the "ideological heresies" of Czechoslovak and Yugoslav reformers were published in all Polish mass communication media.[20] This time, however, various pseudo-scholars of the "pure Marxist brand" were held firmly in check, while the main task was assigned to more reputable economists, who (by and large) took good care not to rock the reformist boat too much. Thus, Hungary's economic model was not challenged at all, while the Czechoslovak and Yugoslav reformers were merely reproached (often more in sorrow than in anger) for going too far, too soon. There were also—needless to say—some obligatory attacks on the "revisionist theories of Ota Sik,"[2 1] but, on the whole, the criticism was seldom vicious or abusive. By October 1968, this new series of anti-reformist articles was discontinued rather abruptly, obviously on orders from the very top.

IV

There were two basic reasons why the open season on economic reformers had come to an end. The first was a definite shift in the political balance of power within the party establishment; the second was a rapid deterioration of the Polish economy. The combined effect of both factors was to make the ruling elite far more amenable to a fresh dose of economic pragmatism. Thus, the stage was set for a third try at introducing meaningful economic reform in Poland.

The shift in the balance of power was the result of an inconclusive outcome of the factional struggle. The hardliners, led by General Moczar, the powerful boss of the secret police, managed to capture some important positions in the party and state apparatus but failed to oust Gomulka and his close associates. Yet while the power struggle at the top had ended in a virtual stalemate, it did create many opportunities for rapid promotion at the middle and lower echelons—the mass 1968 purge of alleged "Zionists," "revisionists," "leftist opportunists," "rightist opportunists" and others having created many vacancies. In any case, the Gomulka group wanted to shed its image as the "tired old men," and political patronage was the way to do it. The net effect was that, after March 1968, a large number of people in their late thirties and early forties advanced to positions where they could exert real political influence.

In political terms, the appointees could hardly be classified as "liberals," or even "progressives." But they were definitely far less dogmatic than their predecessors, much better educated, and much more conscious of Poland's complex economic problems. Several of them could even be regarded as bona fide economic, agricultural, and financial experts who fully appreciated the pressing need for a more pragmatic approach to the questions of planning and management. Thus, the shift in the party power structure created a favorable political climate for still another program of economic reforms, providing that such a program could be contained within the limits of ideological orthodoxy.

The urgent need for such a program was also evident from the rapidly deteriorating economic situation. Dogmatic preeminence had exacted its usual toll by mismanaging national resources so that by the second half of 1968, the Polish economy found itself in the throes of yet another of its periodic crises. The symptoms were painfully familiar: A huge over-commitment of scarce capital goods, leaving no possibility of finishing more than a fraction of the new construction projects; investment cycles dragging on for years, with original cost estimates greatly exceeded; employment, both in the factories and on the macro-economic scale, well above planned targets; low labor productivity; and a drastic disparity between product mix and effective industrial and consumer demand.[22]

The biggest problem was overspending on new investments. The Polish Five-Year Plan for 1966-1970 originally provided 840 billion zloty for investment purposes. Of this, 40 million zloty were to be kept in reserve to meet unforeseen contingencies. However, by 1969 that reserve was already exhausted and an additional 100 billion zloty had to be found (obviously at the expense of the consumption fund) to cover the rising costs of new construction.[23] Even so, only a limited number of "selected" investment projects were to be completed by the end of 1970. Construction work on the remainder was to be "frozen" or "temporarily suspended."

Elsewhere, too, the return to arbitrary methods of planning and management had played havoc with the original Five-Year Plan targets and estimates. Ever since 1966, employment limits were systematically exceeded, both at the micro-economic and macro-economic levels. By the end of 1968, employment outside agriculture had already reached 9.4 million people,[24] as against the planned target of 9.7 million by the end of 1970.[25] Such substantial over-employment not only tended to drive labor productivity down, but inevitably resulted in a huge, above-plan growth of the wage fund (i.e., the total earnings of those employed in the socialized sector). All those factors, combined with the well-known inflationary impact of over-long investment cycles, created a very severe pressure on the scarce supplies of consumer goods.[26]

Faced with this evidence of the inherent inadequacies of a command economy, the Polish ruling elite decided that henceforth the traditional, extensive methods of promoting economic growth ought to be discarded in favor of intensive ones. This basic policy decision had apparently been made some time prior to the Fifth Party Congress (November 1968), at which it was officially promulgated by Gomulka and other principal speakers. They pointed out, however, that it was too late to introduce any substantive changes during the remaining period of the current Five-Year Plan. Therefore, the new system was to become fully operative in January 1971, while the years 1969-1970 were to be treated as a transitory period, during which the main economic task was "to create appropriate conditions for the reconstruction of the national economy in the next five-year term."[27]

In accordance with this basic policy decision, the Congress resolution devoted a lot of space to the proposed changes in the system of planning and management. Due to the political tendencies of the Congress delegates (who were elected at the time of dogmatic ascendancy) and perhaps also because of lack of time, the reform directives were couched in very general terms which could mean all things to all men. Nevertheless, the Congress resolution might possibly be regarded as a mandate of sorts for elaborating a more cohesive program of economic reform.

After official endorsement of the new policy line by the Fifth Congress, the "Young Turks" within the Party establishment managed to take over the top command posts in the economic superstructure and to initiate a reform-oriented ideological discussion in the mass communication media. In December 1968, in one big sweep, the chairman of the Planning Commission, his two deputies, as well as the chairmen of the Committee on Labor and Wages and of the Committee on Science and Technology were dismissed, while Poland's top planner ever since 1956—Stefan Jedrychowski—was made foreign minister. The management of economic affairs was taken over by a new team composed of younger technocrats and experts. This team was to be supervised at the Politburo level by Boleslaw Jaszczuk, the new economic chief. This mass takeover by the Young Turks was later supplemented by numerous changes at the ministerial level, including the key chairmanship of the Polish National Bank.

At the same time, the Party faithful and the economic *apparatchiki*—so recently exposed to anti-reform diatribes of the dogmatists—were now being re-indoctrinated and conditioned for the forthcoming ideological rehabilitation of the market mechanism, the profit motive, and other instruments of economic pragmatism. The stage for such a rehabilitation campaign was set shortly before the Fifth Party Congress, when a prominent economic reformer, Professor Kurowski, was allowed to publish three articles in a mass-circulation paper, *Zycie Warszawy*, in which he discussed the potentialities of the application of a market mechanism in a Communist-type planned economy.[28] After the political setbacks of the dogmatists at the Congress itself, this rehabilitation of the market gathered momentum. The new ideological forumla was put in a nutshell by Bohdan Glinski, a well-known economic reformer, who wrote:

A great majority of economists in all the socialist countries agree that, at the present stage of development of the socialist economies, the mutual relationship between the plan and the market has changed. According to the new prevailing trend of thought, these two basic concepts, instead of being opposed to one another, are, in fact, complementary.[29]

Paradoxically enough, this was precisely the basic idea permeating Professor Brus' reformist theories, as explained in his noted book on the use of the market mechanism in economic planning.[30] But the new forces in the power structure were not really interested in the rehabilitation of Brus and the other victims of the 1968 witch-hunt. The purpose of their indoctrination campaign was to establish the ideological legitimacy of their own reformist concepts.

V

The time has come to determine more precisely the extent and the directions of the proposed changes in the methodology of planning, as well as in the new procedures of management. As already indicated, the mandate obtained by the protagonists of the new economic system at the November 1968 Party Congress was rather shaky and inconclusive. Hence, it was imperative to spell out at least the broad outlines of the proposed reforms and to establish them as the official party line. This political prerequisite for working out a concrete program of a new system of planning and management was duly achieved at the plenary meeting of the newly elected Central Committee, which unanimously endorsed the new reform program in April 1969.

What were the main features of this reform program? First of all, the methods of constructing the national economic plan were to be completely revised. Under the traditional, monocentric system, a detailed version of the national plan was worked out by the central planners, and the basic indicators of this plan, as well as the production targets, were then passed down the chain of command in the form of mandatory directives. Thus, the central planners set definite and detailed production tasks for the individual ministries, each ministry did the same thing for its subordinate industrial associations (trusts), while the associations divided the work to be done among the individual enterprises. As elsewhere in the Moscow bloc, the central planners not only dictated what was to be produced, but also had complete operational control over the logistics of national planning.

This traditional *modus operandi* was now to be completely reversed. As Gomulka put it at the April 1969 CC Plenum: "From now on the plan will be built from the bottom upwards; from the enterprises, through the associations and the ministries, to the Planning Commission."[31] In more realistic and sophisticated terms, one could say that the planning technique foreseen in this third version of the new economic model was intended to strike a rough balance between the principle of self-determination of production tasks at the enterprise level and the basic needs of the national economy, as predetermined by the ruling elite. Thus—in contrast to the old monocentric methods—the individual enterprises were to be given a real chance to establish their own production goals, instead of simply being told what to produce. True, all those enterprise production plans still had to be approved by the higher echelons in the chain of economic command. But, under the new system, the enterprise managers were to have not only the right but also the duty to propose their own production targets, and they could argue the advantages of their targets over those set by their superiors.

This new *methodology of planning* was explained in more detail by the new economic chief, Jaszczuk, in an authoritative article.[32] The process of preparing a draft of a Five-Year Plan was to begin in the Planning Commission, which had the task of formulating a long-term economic forecast covering the period in question. This document—according to Jaszczuk—had, first of all, to indicate the probable trends of development of the national economy (including changes in technology). Secondly, it should contain reliable estimates of future demand requirements (both in the industrial and in the consumer sector). Finally, it should provide a reliable assessment of the total volume of resources available for fulfilling the tasks envisaged in the plan. This long-term forecast was then to be handed down the chain of economic command until it reached the individual enterprises.

The director of each enterprise, as well as the appropriate organs of the Polish variety of workers' self-management were meant to study this forecast in order to relate it to their own productive potential. Every enterprise was supposed to elaborate its own production plan (or, better still, several alternative versions of it). Those plans were then to be sent to the appropriate industrial association or trust for scrutiny and approval. At this stage, production targets and other aspects of each enterprise's draft plan were to be checked by competent officials of the association to see whether they conformed with the main indicators and basic guidelines of the long-term estimates. (This pertained to such items as the proposed growth of employment and labor productivity, the intended investment expenditure and its purpose, as well as the actual product mix.) All objections raised by the association had to be discussed with the management of the enterprise concerned, with the aim of finding a mutually acceptable solution.[33]

After obtaining the necessary *placet* of the competent association, the draft production plans of the individual enterprises were to become integrated into a single comprehensive plan covering the whole branch of industry. Such plans had, in turn, to be approved by the appropriate ministry, where a similar checking and coordinating procedure would be followed. Subsequently, the ministries were to forward their own composite draft plans to the Planning Commission, where they were to be again compared with the long-term estimates and the national economic indicators. Finally, the Planning Commission had to combine all ministerial-level proposals into the draft of the National Economic Plan.

Such truly Parkinsonian procedure was no doubt rather cumbersome and time-consuming. It is even pertinent to ask whether all this bureaucratic effort involved in preparing, checking, and coordinating hundreds of micro-economic draft plans, would be really worthwhile. Hungary by contrast, has solved the dilemma of striking an equitable balance between the particular interests of individual enterprises and the over-all interests of the national economy in a far less complex and much more efficient manner. Nevertheless, even with all its drawbacks and limitations, the new methodology of Polish planning incorporated in the 1969-70 version of new economic model could still be regarded as a significant improvement, especially when compared with the old patterns of command economy and the initiative-stultifying system of bureaucratic controls.

The main symbol of this break with the principles of a command economy was the major change both in the status and essential functions of the central planners. Under the traditional system, the Planning Commission played a pivotal role not only in the process of planning but also in day-by-day management. Thus, in effect, the central planners used to run the whole economy. By contrast, in the third version of the Polish economic model, the Planning Commission has been assigned a very different and far more peripheral role. First of all, the central planners have been divested of their prerogatives in the sphere of day-to-day management, which from now on was to be the sole concern of ministries, of industrial associations, and of the enterprises themselves. Secondly, the central planners ceased to be directly involved in the process of short and medium-term planning. Instead, the Planning Commission has been transformed into an institution whose primary concern is to be long-term forecasting of economic and technological trends.[34]

One has to emphasize, however, that while the central planners have been deprived of the bulk of their former powers in the spheres of short and medium-term planning, as well as operative management and performance control, the supervisory prerogatives of the ministries and industrial associations have been decidedly strengthened. Below the level of the central planners, the old bureaucratic superstructure has not only retained most of its old prerogatives but has acquired many new ones. Thus, one could hardly claim that any meaningful degree of genuine decentralization was involved in the economic reform program devised in the years 1969-70.

The new methodology of planning was, however, only one of the elements of this reform blueprint. The two other key features of this program, elaborated prior to the ouster of Gomulka, were the new principles of investment financing and the ill-fated system of material incentives, which was regarded by its promoters as the backbone of the whole new scheme.

By mid-1969, the new ground rules of *investment financing* had been already clearly defined. Competent authorities stated emphatically that the old practice of free investment grants had to be abandoned in favor of a system of interest-bearing loans administered and supervised through the banking network. A standard interest rate of 3 per cent was to be charged on all such loans, and a complicated system of bonuses and penalties, depending on the progress of the investment project and the ability of the investor to keep within the original cost estimates, has been drawn up.[35]

All this, however, left open the most crucial issue, namely, who (and on what basis) was supposed to make the final choice between the competing claims for the allocation of available investment funds. It has been authoritatively stated that the decisive factor in making such a choice should be "the comparative effectiveness of the investment outlays involved in the available alternatives."[36] But no one has ever explained how this comparative effectiveness was to be objectively measured and by what standards.

However, it was the new system of *material incentives* that proved to be the most controversial feature of the whole reform blueprint. The basic principle of this system was sound enough. What its promoters were aiming at was to provide a direct cause and effect relationship between the economic performance of the given enterprise and the growth of wages and salaries.[37] The general idea was that each year a certain sum of money (the amount of which was to depend on the fulfillment of a number of performance targets) was to be credited to a special fund from which all future wage and salary increases (as well as bonuses) were to be paid.[38] Henceforth, a more efficient enterprise was to be able to pay higher wages and salaries than a less efficient one. This—it was hoped—would give the workers a real stake in the overall economic performance of the enterprise they worked for. Thus, the new system of material incentives was conceived as a break with the old method of arbitrary wage fixing for a whole industry.[39]

But if the basic principles were sound, the essential provisions of the system itself were not. First of all, the criteria established to measure the economic performance of an individual enterprise were so complicated that they were beyond the comprehension not only of an average worker but even of an accomplished bureaucrat.[40] It is sufficient to say that this economic performance was to be measured by one synthetic indicator and at least four sectional performance targets ranging from the coefficient of labor-cost reduction to the rate of technological progress. An elaborate weighting system (so many points for improving the synthetic indicator and so many for implementing each sectional performance target) was established in order to determine the exact amounts of money to be credited to the special fund.[41]

To complicate matters still further, the whole system was replete with various devices for blocking actual wage increases, at least in the short run.[42] In fact, were this system to be implemented as of January 1971, as originally intended, the net effect would be a general *de facto* wage freeze lasting at least until mid-1972. The reason for this is that, according to the implementing order issued by the Polish government, the actual economic results achieved by each enterprise in 1970 are to serve as a base against which all future yearly performances (until 1975) were to be measured and evaluated.[43] Hence, the very earliest that any amount of money could be credited to the special wage-increase fund would be when the complicated accounting process needed to assess progress during 1971 is finished and approved by higher echelons of the economic superstructure.

This built-in wage-freeze feature of the new system of material incentives was by no means accidental. Quite the contrary, it was a deliberate policy decision. By 1970 the economic situation in Poland had deteriorated to such an extent that not only were no funds available for any wage increases, but the powers-that-be had to resort to mass dismissals involving some 200,000 workers, as well as to severe restrictions on new hirings. In fact, the original version of the 1971-75 plan (approved a few weeks before the ouster of Gomulka) provided for residual unemployment of about half a million people.[44]

Thus, by the end of 1970, the Polish workers were facing the prospect of an enforced wage freeze and of growing unemployment. There were also acute shortages of meat, milk, fats, and certain consumer durables. Then, in December 1970, came the blow: a decree on price increases. The patience of the Polish workers was obviously exhausted, and sporadic strikes and street demonstrations snowballed into a threat of a general strike. The party leadership capitulated, and Gomulka and his close associates were ousted.

The downfall of Gomulka was followed by a public condemnation of his "ill-considered" economic policies. And, from a formal point of view, this also meant the end of the third version of the Polish economic model, since a new leadership—as is customary in communist states—must start with its own program in order to "legitimize" its position. So is it with the Gierek leadership. After the socio-political impact of the workers' revolt which brought down Gomulka was officially assessed by the Party Central Committee at its February 1971 Plenum, a special top-level commission was formed in March to prepare "a comprehensive program of economic reforms."[45] This program, according to the pre-Congress Guidelines, was to be presented at the Sixth Party Congress in December 1971 for discussion and final approval.[46]

But contrary to this definite commitment, no such report was presented, and the Congress delegates were merely informed that the commission preparing the new economic model was still continuing its work.

However, the reforms were one of the chief topics of discussion at the Sixth Congress, although the subject was treated in a rather general way. Nevertheless, both from the keynote speeches and from the more authoritative voices in the discussion, the following highlights did emerge:[47]

(1) There was general agreement that reforms are necessary, and that they should go in the general direction of a more decentralized economic model allowing much more scope for initiative from below.

(2) To avoid the mistakes made in the past, the new model should be introduced all at once and not piecemeal, as in previous attempts.

(3) The role of the central planners should be limited to (a) decision making involving basic proportions of future economic

development; (b) determining the general objectives of long-term economic policies; and (c) long-term economic forecasting. On the other hand, the central planners would have no say in operative decision making, which would be left to enterprises and industrial associations.

(4) The enterprises should be given much greater freedom of action, especially in the sector of wage-determination. It is still unclear, however, what will be the relationship between enterprises and industrial associations and to what extent the intermediate level superstructure would be permitted to interfere in the operative decisions of enterprise directors. It seems probable that the new model will opt for an organizational structure that will vary according to the specific conditions in a given branch of industry.

What will actually happen is, of course, uncertain. But one has good reasons to expect a fourth version of the Polish economic reform, yet what form it will take nobody could know for sure.

Notes

1. Cf. the two relevant official "Theses of the Economic Council," in *Zycie Gospodarcze*, June 2 and Dec. 22-29, 1957, as well as the draft decrees on workers' councils and workers' self-management in *Trybuna Ludu*, Nov. 1, 1956 and Oct. 11, 1958. For more details see my *Economic Reforms in Eastern Europe* (Detroit: Wayne State University Press, 1968), chapter 2, "Poland: The Frustrated Pioneer."

2. See his "How Do I Visualize the Polish Economic Model," *Trybuna Ludu*, Dec. 31, 1957. It should also be stressed that this period coincided with Gomulka's assurance that private farming would be maintained and expanded so as to gradually give market forces their say in agriculture as well.

3. This hostile pressure was eventually admitted by the official Polish media. See W. Brus, "Some General Remarks on the Changes in the System of Planning and Management," *Gospodarka Planowa*, Nov. 1966, p. 11.

4. The Economic Council became moribund in mid-1959, although it was not formally dissolved until the end of 1962.

5. In October, 1959, E. Szyr, the chief planner of the pre-October era, and J. Tokarski, the Minister of Machine Industry at the time of the Poznan uprising, were appointed deputy premiers (for economic affairs), while T. Gede was made deputy chairman of the Planning Commission.

6. Cf. "AR," "Increased Tasks and Prerogatives of the Planning Commission," *Trybuna Ludu*, Jan. 5, 1960.

7. The Theses published by *Ksiazka i wiedza*, March 1964.

8. The Resolution in *Trybuna Ludu*, June 25, 1964; the decree of July 29, 1964, in *Monitor Polski*, Aug. 18, 1964; the Decree of March 10, 1965 (provisions summarized) in *Trybuna Ludu*, April 3, 1965; speech by Poland's chief of planning; S. Jedrychowski, at the Fourth Plenum of the Central Committee, *Trybuna Ludu*, July 27, 1965.

9. For further details of this second version of the Polish reform blueprint, see my "Economic Reform in Poland," *East Europe*, July 1965.

10. July 30, 1967.

11. Ibid.

12. W. Iskra, "Ideological Backbone of the Economy," *Trybuna Ludu*, April 23, 1968.

13. For instance, Professor Brus lost his job in April 1968 and was transformed into an "unperson." Others, like Professor Laski, were forced to emigrate to Israel.

14. M. Krajewski, "Socialist Democracy and Market Socialism," *Trybuna Ludu*, March 29, 1968.

15. Ibid.

16. W. Iskra, "Ideological Backbone," *Trybuna Ludu*, April 23, 1968.

17. Ibid.

18. "Ideological Problems of the Economy," *Zycie Gospodarcze*, June 9, 1968.

19. Ibid.

20. Cf. a series of five articles under the joint title "Yugoslav Economic Reforms in Practice" by J. Wilkowski and M. Zalewski, *Trybuna Ludu*, Sept. 8, 9, 10, 11, 12, 1968; S. Chelstowski and Z. Wyczesany, "Yugoslavia after the Economic Reform—Stagnation and its Results," *Zycie Gospodarcze*, Sept. 8, 1968; A. Bober, "Two Tendencies" and "Yearning for the Market," *Zycie Warszawy*, Aug. 28 and 29, 1968; S. Albinowski, "The Czechoslovak Economic Model—An Evolution towards the Past," *Trybuna Ludu*, Aug. 30 and Sept. 2, 1968.

21. Cf. two articles by J. Chlopecki, "The Father of the Czechoslovak Reform" and "Radical Reformers," *Kierunki*, Sept. 22 and 29, 1968.

22. All those ills of the Polish economy were explicitly enumerated in the Report of the Central Committee presented at the Fifth Party Congress. Cf. *Nowe Drogi*, December 1968, pp. 7-11.

23. Cf. Gomulka's concluding speech at the Second Central Committee Plenum, *Trybuna Ludu*, April 9, 1969.

24. *Biuletyn Statystyczny*, 3:8. (The Polish 1966-1970 Plan was based on the assumption that employment would grow at an annual rate of some 300,000.)

25. *Nowe Drogi*, Dec. 1966, pp. 6-7.

26. G. Pisarski, "The Achievements and Difficulties of Dynamic Growth," *Zycie Gospodarcze*, Dec. 22-29, 1968.

27. "Resolution of the Fifth Congress of the PUWP," *Trybuna Ludu*, Nov. 21, 1968.

28. S. Kurowski, "The Problems of the Plan and of the Market," *Zycie Warszawy*, Oct. 2, 3, and 5, 1968.

29. B. Glinski, "The Role of the Market in Planned Economy," *Gospodarka Planowa*, Vol. 12, 1968.

30. W. Brus, *General Questions Concerning the Functioning of a Socialist Economy* (Warsaw, 1961).

31. Gomulka's concluding speech at the Second Plenum, *Nowe Drogi*, May 1969, pp. 51-60.

32. B. Jaszczuk, "The Policy of Intensive Development," *Zycie Gospodarcze*, June 1, 1969.

33. Premier (now head of state) Cyrankiewicz's remarks at a special seminar for high-level officials of the economic apparatus. *Trybuna Ludu*, May 15, 1969.

34. Jaszczuk's speech at the budgetary session of the Polish Parliament, *Trybuna Ludu*, Dec. 22, 1968.

35. S. Majewski, "Changes in the Methods of Investment Financing," *Gospodarka Planowa*, August, 1969.

36. S. Kuzinski, "On the Criteria of Choice in the Investment Sector in the Years 1971-1975," *Nowe Drogi*, October 1969.

37. B. Jaszczuk's report at the Fifth Central Committee Plenum in *Trybuna Ludu*, May 20, 1970.

38. Z. Szeliga, "The Reform of Wages," *Polityka*, March 21, 1970.

39. "The Main Features of the New System of Material Incentives," an interview with M. Krukowski, Chairman of the Committee for Manpower and Wages, *Trybuna Ludu*, March 28, 1970.

40. The faults of the new system were fully acknowledged after the ouster of Gomulka. (See B. Fick, "The System of Incentives," *Zycie Gospodarcze*, Feb. 7, 1971.)

41. Z. Szeliga, op. cit.

42. B. Fick, "The System of Incentives," *Zycie Gospodarcze*, Feb. 7, 1971.

43. Cf. "Decision of the Council of Ministers and the General

Council of the Trade Unions on the Implementation of the System of Material Incentives," *Trybuna Ludu*, July 7, 1970.

44. H. Krol, "Intensive Development Versus Employment," *Trybuna Ludu*, Feb. 15, 1971.

45. *Trybuna Ludu*, Feb. 15, 1971.

46. The Guidelines, "On the Further Socialist Development of the Polish People's Republic," adopted by the Party Plenum on September 4, 1971, were published in a brochure by *Trybuna Ludu* (1971).

47. Proceedings of the Sixth Congress, *Trybuna Ludu*, Dec. 7-12, 1971.

7

Rumania: The Laggard

Claus-D. Rohleder

I

Inadequate economic performance—a widely shared basic problem in the countries of Eastern Europe—has prompted the introduction of reforms whose timing and scope have varied according to each country's stage of development. A number of these countries preceded Rumania in embarking on economic reforms in an effort to solve the problems that a rigid plan creates in a more sophisticated economy. Rumania not only delayed her reforms but has thus far only marginally renovated her orthodox economic structure, despite the fact that by the mid-1960s Rumanian economists and official planners certainly must have observed that the country was exhausting the advantages of extensive development. Evidently, the necessity for economic reform did not seem too pressing, and so only modest and inconspicuous attempts were made to adjust to the new realities, which left the centralized model basically intact.[1]

The reasons for clinging so persistently to centralism are both historically and politically motivated. Historically, the country has never known a true democratic system, having been ruled almost exclusively by royal or military central authority. After the communist seizure of power, the party leaders, like the generals and monarchs before them, pursued a policy of strict political centralization and thorough state control. Although a cautious liberalization has been noticeable from time to time, its impact has been more on the personal life of the citizens than on the economic and political life of the country as a whole and is primarily a function of the degree of the party leadership's self-confidence at any given moment.[2]

Speculation concerning the possibility of economic reforms has surfaced time and again ever since the mid-1960s when Rumania embarked on her rather independent foreign policy. Although over the years more changes have been carried out than is generally known, and although Bucharest quietly took notice of the discussions of reform proposals in other bloc countries, Rumania has not yet discussed or codified in any comprehensive way the core issues of economic reforms—except in a few specific instances, such as in its discussions of price reform. These discussions concerned a reorganization of cost and price levels and not the introduction of a price system reflecting true cost and scarcity prices. Nevertheless, criticism of the present price system is not without importance, because the elimination of distorted cost-price relationships and the introduction of more realistic prices (mainly in terms of their absolute level) could develop a now lacking cost-consciousness.

Following the principle that one should theorize less and experiment more, the Rumanians have indeed taken several "perfectioning" steps (an official term often used to describe reform measures), principally in the field of economic planning and management, but the suitability of these measures is in most cases determined *ex post facto* in discussions among experts. The call for a planned improvement or "perfectioning" of all sectors of the economy suggests that greater importance may eventually be attached to actual discussion of the reforms. This could mean a transition from the "perfectioning" to the reform process being followed in other socialist countries of Eastern Europe.[3]

II

As early as the Ninth Congress of the Rumanian Communist Party of July 1965, when the Five-Year Plan for 1966-1970 was approved, the leading party and state functionaries began to criticize existing features of the economic system and to suggest the need for reform, first of all in the system of industrial planning and management. However, when measures relating to a reform of the economic administration were announced by Party Chief Ceausescu at the Central Committee Plenum in December 1966, it was not clear whether or not they would lead to a real decentralization and debureaucratization of the economy (and especially of the role of industrial enterprises).[4] It was exactly one year later, in December 1967, that the National Conference of the Rumanian Communist Party (equivalent to an extraordinary party congress) passed the so-called "directives for perfectioning the management and planning of the national economy in accordance with the demands of the new stage of socialist development in Rumania," (hereinafter referred as Directives) which had been approved in October 1967 by a Central Committee plenum and which still represent the basic Rumanian "blueprint" for reform.[5] One must hasten to add that the introductory chapter itself makes it unmistakably clear that this was not (as had been expected) a real reform, that is, a departure from former dogma, that—to use the exact language—the directives "do not mean discarding the centralistic principle of economic planning"; they mean instead "a search for suitable ways and means to manage and organize the economy" so as to achieve "greater perfection of the planning system."[6]

The great variety of measures aimed primarily at improving general economic effectiveness affected all sectors of the economy; yet they did not question the validity of the central economic plan and its central coordinating function. Therefore, any kind of self-regulating effect of the market was rejected, so that a comprehensive reorientation of the price system could not be expected.[7] It is also interesting to note that the measures outlined in the Directives were not to be carried out immediately but gradually and only after they had been adequately tested. Indeed, the Directives, which must be understood as a preliminary to the planned economic reforms, have been carried out only partially. The deadline for their completion (originally set for the end of 1969) has been postponed for one year, yet—despite some positive steps—their implementation has been lagging.[8]

Limiting outselves to an analysis of the 1967 blueprint, it should be recognized that although the pillars of central planning and party control are not to be shaken, the principal weight in preparing the new plan is to be shifted to the basic economic units (enterprises), so as to be better able to take into account relevant impulses coming from the lower levels upwards. The enterprises would thus be enabled to influence the output expected of them within the framework of their "economic self-management," including the use of contracts.[9] This tendency toward enterprise self-management and the resulting involvement of the workers in enterprise operations has considerable importance for the economic system in Rumania, although its significance should not be exaggerated and although workers' representatives, rather than the workers directly, are to be given such rights in the larger enterprises. Despite the fact that Rumania has not gone so far in this respect as Yugoslavia, where self-management is a reality, she alone in the Eastern bloc has institutionalized the right of workers' participation.[10] Also in the field of wages and salaries, an innovation of the 1967 blueprint was the provision for bonuses tied to the fulfillment of planned profits; a modification of these original provisions was made in 1970, relating the bonus fund to actually achieved profits, and not to plan fulfillment.[11]

The enterprises were also given wider scope in financial matters. All enterprise investments, unless involving the construction of entire plants, are to be financed by enterprise savings and/or with the help of interest-bearing bank credits. The existing practice according to which all the earnings of the enterprises are surrendered to the state and all enterprise expenditures are financed by the state, is to be discarded. In the future, the state budget will finance only new plants. Financial decisions concerning replacements and other minor investments will now be made autonomously by the enterprises themselves.[1][2]

The most important step aimed officially at freeing the economy from bureaucratic management is the creation of industrial combines ("centrals") or trust groupings. These institutions, comparable in Western terminology to "branch holding companies," are to constitute an intermediate level between the branch ministries and the individual enterprises. Experimentation with these industrial combines indicates that some difficulties have been encountered in setting them up, to the extent that Ceausescu himself deemed it necessary to postpone their implementation on a wide scale until the beginning of the new Five-Year Plan (1971-1975). These industrial combines, in a sense the nuclei of the economic reform, may be organized either on a horizontal or vertical basis. In the former case, they link a group of enterprises with identical or similar outputs; in the latter, they combine enterprises at different stages of production.[1][3]

Since the industrial and branch ministries have delegated many of their operational functions to the industrial combines and are to be principally concerned with plan fulfillment and with global plan analysis and coordination, the various combines have become a link—not only institutional and hierarchical but definitely also material and functional—between the individual enterprise and the ministry. It is their task to devise and supervise the plans of their respective branches. Moreover, they are also in charge of inner-plant problems of planning and financing, the specification of outputs, the organization of production, and coordination among enterprises.

Since the directives came into force, about 200 industrial combines and several "industrial groups" have been formed, all of which ostensibly elaborate their own short and long-term plans within the framework of overall state planning and allot binding tasks to their subordinate enterprises. As a typical example of such formations, let us take the four industrial combines and one industrial group that are subordinate to the Ministry of Machine Building. The four combines include one for electronics and automation (comprising 12 enterprises in Bucharest); a second for chemicals and refinery equipment (six plants in Bucharest); a third for trucks and tractors (consisting of truck and tractor works and diverse auxiliary workshops in Brasov); and a fourth for shipbuilding (comprising all shipyards in Galati). The "industrial group" involves railroad car construction (four plants in Arad). Similarly, the Ministry of Electric Power is responsible for industrial combines in charge of electric and thermal power production in Bucharest (i.e., all of Rumania's power stations) as well as power transmission and distribution (the electricity supply grid in Bucharest). An industrial combine for coal mining in Petroseni coordinates the Schil Valley mines and is controlled by the Ministry of Mining. The industrial combine for metal products and coke was established near the iron works at Hunedoara; the petro-chemical "group" Borzesti (head offices in Gheorghiu-Dej) was established under the Ministry for the Chemical Industry.[14]

The industrial combines (as well as other economic units—down to the enterprise level) have been given also a greater role in foreign trade, so as to achieve a more satisfactory adjustment of domestic outputs to the requirements of foreign markets. Although the state monopoly and the final say of the central authority are not affected, combines can be authorized to conclude agreements with foreign trading partners and are supposed to oversee exports and imports by branches, in the hope that bureaucratic red tape in foreign trade will be cut. Until now, import plans were executed exclusively by the appropriate foreign trade association of the Ministry of Foreign Trade, after these plans were approved by the responsible office in the branch ministry, and coordinated by the Planning Commission before they reached the factory. The red tape was just as tangled on the export side. From now on also industrial combines are to be responsible for the foreign sales of enterprises under their jurisdiction, pending the granting of a permit by the Foreign Trade Ministry. Enterprises will be held responsible for fulfilling their export plans, regardless of their success in meeting general output targets. Moreover, they are to engage in market research in foreign countries in collaboration with the official foreign trade organs; they are to maintain their own sales offices and warehouses abroad and to appoint permanent or temporary representatives in various foreign countries. A final important provision of the new Law relates to economic cooperation with third countries. Rumania seems to be following the Yugoslav example of allowing joint-ownership ventures, in which even Western firms may furnish up to 49 percent of the paid-in capital and with the opportunity to export most of their earnings.[15]

On the whole, overall planning in Rumania will continue to operate on the basis of five-year plans, with only some special sectors like power, geology, and scientific research spread out over two five-year periods. However, there has been a growing interest in longer-term planning and forecasting. The Tenth Party Congress of 1969 issued ten-year guidelines, supplemented by a ten-year extension until 1990; and a special Commission on Economic and Social Forecasting, composed of the top party and state leadership, is to prepare for some sectors data and eventual guidelines extending until the year 2000.[16]

As to plan fulfillment, only those indicators are to remain in force which "express fundamental objectives." On the basis of the tasks assigned to them by the state plan, the industrial combines will prescribe specific tasks for their subordinate enterprises, using the following indicators: gross output and product mix; quantities to be supplied to domestic and foreign markets; domestic and imported raw and other materials; productivity of labor; total wage fund; maximum size of labor force; average wage; cost per 1,000 lei of output and production cost of the most important products; volume of accumulation in proportion to capital; volume of payments to the state; volume of investments and list of investment items.[17] But, in actual fact, these criteria have remained substantially on paper.

III

In summary, the Rumanian reform blueprint, as contained in the Directives approved by the Plenum of the Central Committee and sanctioned by the National Conference of the Rumanian Communist Party, show that Rumania—like the Soviet Union, the German Democratic Republic, and Poland—has decided on the conservative road to economic reform. The decisions of 1967 and their gradual implementation aim at more effective planning and control; yet, not as in Hungary, they do not attempt to combine elements of the market mechanism with the socialist economy. Ceausescu himself made it clear that the Rumanian leadership is "against those theories . . . which hold that the regulation of economic and social life should be left to the discretion of the market, to the law of supply and demand."[18] And a new Price-and-Wage Law, while providing for frequent revisions of prices and wages so as to have them better reflect social costs and profitability by also introducing land rent and interest on capital, made it clear that the center will continue decreeing all prices and wages.[19] As a result, the Rumanian measures, which are designed to rationalize and increase economic effectiveness rather than to decentralize, promise systematic improvements but also raise fears that the disadvantages of half-hearted decentralization measures will sooner or later become conspicuous.

Nevertheless, a beginning seems to have been made to try and dispel misgivings concerning inadequacies and errors in the existing economic system. Rumania has initiated a process of "debureaucratization"–albeit not a true decentralization process–by placing younger experts in responsible managerial and administrative positions as well as by somewhat hesitant "improvement measures." And the next Five-Year Plan (1971-75) is to be organized in accordance with the Directives. Ceausescu, after having realized the dangers of letting party leaders combine state and economic functions, has renewed his urgings against "excessive centralism," and new regulations call for greater management responsibility and economic efficiency.[20] It should also be added that, contrary to the reforms in other Soviet-bloc countries, economic changes in Rumania are free of explosive ideological matter, and the new economic course is not intended to supply others with an example to follow, which may be a warranty against sudden reversals of the slow pace of Rumanian economic reforms.

Notes

1. Thus, the Party Congress of July 1965 emphasized the growing importance of the state in developing the national economy, including agriculture, and Ceausescu called the Central Committee of the communist party "the general staff responsible for building a socialist society" in his speech before the December 1966 Central Committee Plenum. Cf. H. Siegert, *Rumaenien heute* (Rumania Today) (Vienna and Duesseldorf, 1966).

2. Ibid.

3. See Gregory Grossman, "The Communist Economic Reforms," A Report for the Sub-Committee on International Trade, Committee on Banking and Currency, House of Representatives, Washington, D.C., March 1, 1967, pp. 43 to 54; and his "Economic Reforms: A Balance Sheet," in *Problems of Communism*, November-December 1966, pp. 43-55.

4. Translated in *Neuer Weg*, Dec. 27, 1966. See also C.-D. Rohleder, "Die rumaenische Wirtschafsentwicklung–Beginn einer neuen Phase," in K. Thalheim and H.H. Hoehmann, eds. *Wirtschafts-reformen in Osteuropa* (Economic Reforms in Eastern Europe) (Cologne, 1968), p. 238 ff.

5. *Radio Bucharest*, Dec. 6, 1967, and Law No. 22 of 1967. (English text in "Rumanian Press Survey," no. 728, *Radio Free Europe Research*, Dec. 20, 1967.)

6. Ibid.

7. See Jon Dobrescu, "Die Rolle der Finanzen, des Kredits, und der Preise im Wirtschaftsprozess der Industrieunternehmen" (The Role of Finances, Credits, and Prices in the Economic Process of Industrial Enterprises), in *Economia Intreprinderii Industriale* (Bucharest, 1968), p. 309.

8. Cf. Law No. 48 of December 29, 1969, extending the deadline to December 31, 1970.

9. Cf. The Law on Economic Contracts of 1969 (*Buletinul Oficial*, no. 154, Dec. 29, 1969), supplemented by a Ministerial Decree (ibid., no. 68, June 20, 1970) that made contracts precede the preparation of the enterprise plans and, of course, central plan formulation. Sharp criticism was leveled at the inadequate implementation of these contracts in 1970 (See *Viata Economica*, December 1970).

10. See appropriate acts in *Buletinul Oficial*, no. 42 of April 3, 1968 and *Munca*, Oct. 23, 1971. Useful comment in *Neue Zuercher Zeitung*, May 31, 1969 and Henry Schaefer, "Collective Management in Rumania," *Radio Free Europe Research*, Feb. 24, 1972. A new and interesting feature is the provision to rely on action taken by the employees' collective if an enterprise fails to improve its performance.

11. Cf. *Agerpres*, Feb. 21, 1970.

12. Cf. *Osteuropaeische Rundschau*, Nov. 11, 1967, and nos. 2 and 6, 1969; also *Handelsblatt*, Oct. 3-4, 1969. Subsequent regulation has introduced punitive interest rates to encourage efficiency and responsibility. (*Viata Economica*, no. 31, June 31, 1970).

13. Ibid.

14. Cf. *Handelsblatt*, ibid.

15. Text of the Law in *Neuer Weg*, Mar. 19, 1971. Cf. also the author's "Rumaenien" (Rumania) in J. Meier and J. Hawlowitsch, eds., *Die Aussenwirtschaft Suedosteuropas* (Southeastern Europe's Foreign Commerce) (Cologne, 1970) and J. Bethkenhagen, "Zur Aussenwirtschaftsreform in Rumaenien," (On the Foreign-Trade Reforms in Rumania), in *Vierteljahreshefte zur Wirtschaftsforschung* (Quarterly Papers on Economic Research), no. 3, 1971.

16. *Scanteia*, July 8, 1971.

17. See *Osteuropaeische Rundschau*, no. 11, 1967, p. 32, ff.

18. Speech delivered at the 50th anniversary of the Rumanian party in May 1971.

19. See *Buletinul Oficial*, no. 154, Dec. 16, 1971.

20. Cf. *Scanteia*, Feb. 13 and 25, 1971.

8

Yugoslavia: The Pioneer Still Leads

Johann Hawlowitsch

General Aspects of the Transformation Process

Within the framework of the economic and social changes in the socialist states of Eastern Europe, Yugoslavia occupies a special place. It is the only socialist country which has passed through a very animated and unparalleled transformation from a centrally directed Soviet-type economy to a more or less decentralized "socialist market economy."[1] It is not absolutely necessary to trace all the details of this process of transformation in order to go into the question as to whether or to what extent the Yugoslav reforms constitute a rapprochement with the "market system" of the West. In any case, the reorganization has not yet been completed, and many of the numerous problems that arose in the past are still present today and are even apt to re-emerge quite suddenly, to become more visible and, as a result, to lend themselves to a more precise analysis.

The specific Yugoslav economic and social order was never—and is not today—a blueprint of a ready-made ideology or a closed system concept. Characteristic for the country's transformation process, which has been going on for about 20 years, is rather the fact that, as a rule, it was real-life problems arising from concrete economic and political practice that motivated the experimental search for pragmatic solutions. The most important stages of this development are as follows:

Yugoslavia began to adopt the Stalinist political and economic model in 1946, earlier than the other states within the Soviet sphere of influence. For the next four years, the economic system bore the well-known features of a centrally planned and directed economy of the Soviet type. Meanwhile, the Cominform conflict of 1948 caused Yugoslavia's break with the Soviet bloc. The fact that even after the break the Yugoslav leadership continued to develop the political power apparatus and central planning along Stalinist lines suggests that this event was not directly responsible for the basic reforms

123

initiated only two years later. To be sure, the subsequent ideological breakaway from the Soviet bloc in 1950 was a precondition for these reforms, which were necessitated by the economic difficulties created by over-centralization.

The year 1950 is the birthdate of the present system. It was then that workers' self-management was introduced, while detailed central economic planning—incompatible with that principle—began to be dismantled step by step. Two years later, in 1952, the "Law on the Planned Direction of the Economy," which officially marked the transition to indicative macro-economic planning (based on so-called "Social Plans" of the Federation, the Republics, and the Communes), was a further step toward decentralizing economic decision-making, toward filtering some of this power down to the local commune and enterprise levels.[2]

After a two-year transitional period (1952-53), the system introduced in 1952 was institutionalized by a number of legal acts early in 1954. The system of centrally prescribed compulsory indicators was eliminated. Decisions affecting factor inputs, supplies, and sales, as well as to some extent the composition of managerial staff, were transferred down to the enterprise level. However, the state (or regional authorities) continued to control investment and distribution by direct or in some cases indirect methods. Investments were financed largely from the center by way of credits from the General Investment Fund of the Federation. Practically all profits earned by the enterprises went to the Federal Investment Fund and to the budgets of the local communes in the form of profit and turnover taxes. The enterprises were left with only a small portion of the profits, to be used for investments in spare parts and for bonuses to the workers and employees.

This economic system, although frequently modified, remained fundamentally the same until the reform of 1965. Decentralization and recentralization measures at the enterprise as well as communal level alternated on and off during the 1950s and even the early 1960s. They must be understood as a reflection of the power struggle between reformist and orthodox groups in the party leadership, and as attempts to cope with specific economic problems. The reforms of 1961 are a case in point.

Thus, at the beginning of 1961, several elements of the existing system were modified in order to remove the structural disproportions that had developed in the meantime. The enterprises were authorized to put a larger share of their profits to their own use so as to increase worker motivation and to make investments more profitable. Decentralization of the banking system was accompanied by an enlarged scope of credit. Taken together, these measures generated strong inflationary tendencies, due to a high propensity to invest, and to substantial wage increases. Also, the partial liberalization of foreign trade helped to produce steadily rising import surpluses. In order to remove these fundamental disequilibria, various measures were adopted in 1962 which again slowed down the liberalization and decentralization process.

This brief survey of Yugoslavia's over-all political and economic development since 1950 gives the impression of a struggle to attain a more efficient social and economic order by means of more or less *ad hoc* measures. The process of experimentation, the search for a Yugoslav road, seems to have been brought to a standstill, at least for the time being, with the new Constitution of 1963. The reforms carried out since then constitute a logical, sometimes radical, translation of the Constitution's relatively clearly conceived ideas of organizing economic, social, and in part, even political life.[3] However, progress has been made substantially more difficult by the fact that, although concepts of the future economic and social order—at least in their fundamentals—are present in the Constitution, the practical experience, and to some extent even the necessary theoretical background for realizing such concepts, are lacking. Because of this, it is understandable why even the extensive changes initiated in 1965 were unable to produce a more definitive structure of the economy.

The economic reform of 1965[4] initiated a process whose consequences cannot yet be fully perceived. The basic idea of these most recent reforms is to transfer economic decision-making to the enterprises even in matters of investment, price, and distribution policy, while "social" ownership of the means of production is to be maintained as a matter of principle. Guidance of the economic process is to occur mainly through the market and price mechanism. The state would limit its influence on the decisions of the individual economic units almost exclusively to measures that are compatible with the market (or compatible with the system). Moreover, the Yugoslav economy is to be integrated with the world economy through a gradual liberalization of its foreign trade system. One hopes thereby to overcome long-term structural and short-term cyclical difficulties.

Even this short summary of the over-all development, unique in economic history, reveals that the Yugoslav economic system has already moved some distance away from the model of a centrally administered economy of the Soviet type and is approaching a system that may be described as a "socialist market economy with workers' self-management." In the following sections we shall explain where, in the essential elements of the Yugoslav social and economic order (especially since 1965), the friction points, dangers, and opportunities arise when translating formal programs into reality. The study of these questions may help us conclude whether a socialist market economy of the Yugoslav type is possible and viable, and whether a rapprochement with the Western market economies has taken place or—if not—whether there is reason to believe that it will take place.

Characteristics and Functioning of the Yugoslav Economic System

Ownership

In Yugoslavia the means of production are "socialized." This specific concept of ownership—as against "state ownership"—is justified by the fact that the power of the state must be restricted. This power, which gives the state a quasi-monopolistic position—it is officially argued—can only be restricted by transferring the rights of ownership (primarily the right to dispose of the means of production and profits) to the immediate producers. The extent of economic freedom depends on the scope of these rights of disposal: the Yugoslav enterprises are almost entirely free to dispose of the resources transferred to them by the administration. The right of the state to interfere with ownership rights is limited essentially to control or supervision. Private property of acquired capital is permissible in certain areas:

(1) In crafts and services, where a private owner may employ a maximum of 6 persons, in addition to the owner's family. Most recently, private undertakings were decreed admissible also in the restaurant and tourist businesses, as well as in some branches of retail trade;

(2) In agriculture, where private ownership is particularly important, eighty-five per cent of all farmland being owned privately. The size of a single holding is, however, limited to 10 hectares (about 25 acres) and measures in practice about 3.3 hectares on the average. Since 1967, private farmers have had free access to the market and are allowed to sell their produce directly to retailers. This privilege should not be overrated, however, because the purchase price of most farm products continues to be fixed or controlled, and the agricultural cooperatives have a practical demand monopoly (monop-

sony) in remote parts of the country. Nevertheless, Yugoslavia, in developing the institution of "general agricultural cooperatives," has succeeded in creating an organization offering private farmers a certain inducement to cooperate with the authorities. Although the private sector now has greater freedom of action, its over-all economic importance has been somewhat reduced over the past few years. While the private sector accounted for 33.2 per cent of the national income in 1957, its share dropped to only 19.9 percent in 1966.[5]

If we take a closer look at what is called "social" ownership, it appears that the exact theoretical meaning of the term continues to be widely disputed in Yugoslav jurisprudence and must be understood in relation to the institution of "workers' self-management." Within this institution, the workers employed in an enterprise (the "workers' collective") have usufructuary rights and limited rights of disposal of the enterprise's means of production. No property relations exist between the enterprise and the workers' collective, because the workers are what may be called "collective entrepreneurs" who manage resources owned by society. As far as relations with third parties are concerned, however, there is a relationship to society (that is, the state, the regional authorities, and other "social" organizations) whereby the legal *"imperium"* of these bodies limits the right of disposal of the workers' collective or the enterprise. Decisive importance must be attached to these hierarchical relationships and to the limits of the right of disposal.[6]

In the first place, the obligation to protect the socially-owned means of production determines the principle of capital preservation. Strict regulations apply in this matter. Fixed capital may not be converted into working capital; fixed capital may not be sold in order to cover losses; and depreciation allowances may be used only for investment in fixed capital. These rules, while necessary to protect social property, have very negative consequences for the individual enterprises as well as for the economy as a whole.[7]

Secondly, the specific relationship between ownership of the means of production and the right of disposal has a decisive influence on enterprise behavior. When some authors[8] interpret collective ownership as formal "social" ownership distinct from the right of disposal of the means of production (the entrepreneur, in Schumpeter's sense, is also not necessarily dependent upon an individualist ownership system) and draw the conclusion that, consequently, a socialist economic system is not *ipso facto* incompatible with decentralized planning, they may be right. But when they use the joint-stock corporation as an example to prove their contention, they are not entirely correct, because the interrelationship in Yugoslavia between ownership and right of disposal creates different interest groups that pursue different goals, and these groups have a decisive influence on the attitude of the managers. The managers of a Yugoslav enterprise are indeed responsible to the owner, that is, to "society," yet they are not remunerated for successful management by this owner and—if at all—by the workers.

The conflict of interests deriving from a system of ownership has different effects in the different economic systems. Thus—unlike in a capitalist system—the Yugoslav manager, if he is not motivated by idealistic notions about the welfare of society, will try to maximize the workers' income within the limits of his responsibility toward the state. This influences his capital investment decisions. If credits cannot be repaid, there is little opportunity to fall back on the assets of the enterprise. Therefore, managers prefer to rely on the anonymous owner, that is, on society (the local commune, in most cases). This may be one of the reasons for the high indebtedness of Yugoslav enterprises.

Another important problem that must be mentioned in this connection cannot be easily explained by the ownership concept. The economist is interested in the totality of assets, which includes not only material objects (means of production, in the first place) but also all working capital and such items as profits derived either competitively or because of monopolistic power. For this reason it would be better to operate with the over-all asset concept rather than with the means of production only, because the workers are given not only the means of production to use and partly dispose of, but the whole enterprise with all its assets. This conclusion raises a number of problems, and one of them, recently under lively discussion in Yugoslavia, is very important: It is the question of the distribution of property, and especially of its impact on the distribution of income. It is a problem that is less acute in other Socialist countries than it is in Yugoslavia, where decentralization very definitely affects the distribution of income.

Managerial Responsibility

As far as economic decision-making is concerned, the present Yugoslav economic system is a mixed system having centralistic as well as decentralistic features. Relationships in this mixed system are difficult to comprehend, because economic rules and reality do not always coincide, and because the numerous laws and regulations are frequently changed or amended. Moreover, several levels participate in decision-making of a macro and micro-economic nature. This is because of the system of self-management, whose principles extend from the economic to the entire social sphere, so that often the same persons or interest groups take part in the decision-making process through their membership in different organizations or boards.

The most important organs of economic initiative are: the state and the regional bodies (responsible for the establishment and dissolution of enterprises); the local and the enterprise party organizations (frequently influencing enterprise decisions), the trade unions (responsible for social policy); the economic chambers and associations; and last but not least, the enterprises and the banks, as decision-making bodies at the micro-economic level.

All enterprises administering society-owned funds are called "economic organizations" in Yugoslav terminology, the most important of them being those in industry. We shall restrict our analysis to the industrial organizations and refer to them as "enterprises" because of the greater familiarity of this term.

These enterprises are juridical "persons" endowed with self-management functions. They are entitled to draw up their economic plans in complete autonomy and are free to determine the volume and structure of production, the input of factors of production, the supply of materials, and the sale of their output. They are also largely independent in their personnel policy: only when appointing the director has the commune a word to say. Direct and indirect restrictions still apply to investment policy, price policy, and profit calculation and distribution. In the latter two fields of enterprise policy, the reform of 1965 extended the scope of enterprise managerial authority and strengthened its financial independence. Problems arising from such a far-reaching decentralization of managerial authority can only be explained in connection with the specific system of enterprise "will formation" in Yugoslavia.

The Yugoslav system is based on the concept of workers' self-management,[9] which today is applied in all fields of human activity, in factories as well as in administrative bodies (even in the universities). This institution was introduced by the Law on Workers' Councils of 1950, which has been repeatedly amended and expanded since then, most recently in connection with the reform of July 1965. The qualitative changes have reached a stage where the legislator prescribes only general norms, while concrete details (including wage rates and profit distribution) are left to the by-laws of each enterprise to regulate. The nature of the self-management principle thus consists in a transfer of economic decision-making, in the areas of production and distribution, to the enterprise itself and to its elective representative organs: workers' council, managing board, and director—comprising the center of enterprise will formation.

The growing independence of enterprises and their various departments places difficult demands on internal enterprise organization. Although the areas of competence are formally and legally delineated, conflicts and certain shifts of power among managerial levels are possible and, in fact, observable in practice. But it will always depend on the concrete situation as to how the self-management principle can be reconciled with the modern methods of management, and to what degree a joint (participatory) management based on democratic principles can in fact be realized. Moreover, the real center of enterprise will formation, and especially the quality of the decisions made, depends on many different factors, such as the educational level of the workers' representatives and the power relations between management and internal as well as local political organizations and communal authorities.[10]

This blueprint of management structure which applies throughout the economy, does not take sufficient account of the particular conditions existing in the individual economic branches and in the different parts of the country. Therefore, in the future the law is merely to stipulate that workers' councils must be formed, while the individual enterprise is to be allowed to constitute its management according to its own specific requirements.

The far-reaching decentralization of economic decision-making—as compared with reforms in other East European countries—subjects the system of workers' self-management to a number of other fundamental questions, among which the following deserve special mention:

(1) The legitimate claim of a worker to employment and consequently to a share of the profit is apt to conflict with enterprise profitability and income maximization. The reform of July 1965 to a certain extent placed economic considerations before political and social goals in this respect: workers may be dismissed when the financial circumstances of the enterprise require it. Yet, many enterprises maintain a special fund to pay temporarily unemployed workers.

(2) The above-mentioned frictions, which are inherent in the system, the conflicts that may arise inside the enterprises, and the positions taken by management (the director or managing board), influence the decisions concerning inputs and sale of output.

(3) The goal of removing the still considerable differences in

economic development in various parts of the country is hardly compatible with a decentralization of investment decisions. In an effort to solve this problem, decisive changes were introduced by the reform of 1965 that took into account the nationalities problem in Yugoslavia: investment funds are no longer re-channeled to the underdeveloped republics through the compulsory surrender of profits, but through monetary, credit, and financial policies.

(4) Profit distribution and use assume a dominant role on account of their wide-reaching effects. Yugoslav enterprises are entitled to use as they wish that proportion of "income" (profit) which remains after deducting business expenses (cost of materials, depreciation, capital tax, and a number of special deductions) and turnover taxes from gross proceeds. The enterprise is allowed to divide this "income," within certain limitations, into "personal income" (wages and workers' share of the profit) and the various enterprise funds (especially those set aside for investment, reserves, and social welfare). While enterprises do not pay profit taxes, the so-called "personal income" portion is subject to very high deductions for taxes, social insurance, housing construction, etc., which must be paid by the enterprise. In 1968, the average burden was nearly thirty-five per cent; the remaining sixty-five per cent of the "income" (profit) can be used largely at the enterprise's discretion, for the guidelines concern only allocations to the reserve fund. In recent years, there is a clear tendency to increase the share of "personal income."[11]

This development gives rise to considerations of a fundamental nature. In an economy of the Yugoslav type, where the workers are at the same time collective entrepreneurs and are largely free to decide how to allocate the net product between consumption and investment, optimal economic growth and economic stability can only be achieved if the state, as the body responsible for over-all economic policy, applies means appropriate to the aims. In our opinion, it is doubtful whether the professed aims of growth and stability may be attained by indirect market-conforming measures alone. Here the limitations and tensions inherent in a socialist market economy become apparent.

The development of self-management, the progressive decentralization of investment, and the call for a rational monetary and credit policy as an instrument of stabilization caused Yugoslavia to reorganize its banking system in 1965,[12] a task begun in early 1966. Except for the National Bank, all other banks may now operate independently within the framework of general credit policy and the Banking Law and are allowed to compete with each other even outside their regions. The banks are organized on the principle of self-management, and on a kind of cooperative basis. The communes and the enterprises are to contribute capital to the bank of their choice, which gives them the right to participate in its management. The weight of their vote depends on the amount of their capital contribution but beyond this is limited so as to assure that financially strong communes and enterprises do not exert undue influence on the banks. In addition, every bank has a credit committee composed exclusively of experts and endowed with the sole responsibility of examining and approving credit applications.

As regards the flexibility of monetary and credit policy, it is the National Bank that is of great importance. As the bank of issue, it is responsible only to Parliament and is not concerned with providing credit for investment or with other banking operations. The National Bank is supposed to regulate the volume of credit and money, primarily through its minimum-reserve and interest-rate policy. Although the communal (local) banks were supposed to have greater independence, their business policy is still influenced largely by the National Bank and the communes. The financing of investments is the almost exclusive responsibility of three special banks that operate only at the federal level (the Investment Bank, the Agricultural Bank, and the Foreign Trade Bank); all are subject to instructions from the center.

This indicates that the problem of organizing the banking and credit system has not yet been solved in the spirit of the latest reforms. As a result, it is difficult to judge how far the banks are actually using their independence to take economic initiatives and, consequently, to know how lasting an influence they might have in the economic life of Yugoslavia.

The Planning System and the Market

The form and the methods of planning were, of course, affected by the progress of decentralization. Until 1965, long-term plans were supplemented by annual economic plans, but the indicators of the annual plans were restricted to macro-economic aggregates and did not prescribe binding targets. Since 1966, however, the federal government, the six republics, and the communes have been elaborating only long-term programs. Cyclical analyses are to be made at shorter intervals, supplying information on the implementation of planned development and permitting economic policy to adjust to a changing situation. This is an entirely new concept of Socialist planning and has nothing in common with planning practices in other East European states.

The most important of all plans is the federal government's "Social Plan," whose significance in directing the economy is disputed even by Yugoslav authors. This plan establishes global macro-economic goals, especially the volume, structure and distribution of the social product, and determines the instruments required to implement these goals. Although these plans do not prescribe concrete targets, their indirect influence on the investment policy of the enterprise is undeniable. They serve the enterprises as points of reference as to anticipated economic policy and development.

In principle, the Yugoslav economy is supposed to be guided by the price mechanism of the market place. This principle is being violated, however, because strong tendencies toward concentration and monopolization persist unchecked, especially in key industries, and because the state still interferes with the autonomy of enterprises via the "social bookkeeping service" and also continues to influence prices through extensive controls.

In the Yugoslav economic system, price policy has an important role in trying to establish economic equilibrium. In principle, enterprises can freely negotiate buying and selling prices by taking into account existing market conditions. However, the state still intervenes in the pricing process in order to counteract inflationary tendencies. In fact, as an emergency anti-inflationary measure, all prices were officially frozen for a six-month period in October 1970. Yet, even before the freeze, alongside governmentally-fixed prices for a minor proportion of output, prices of about half of the industrial products were subject to government controls, a situation which stands in the way of adjusting the price structure to actual supply and demand and also retards technological and economic progress. The system of price controls is so constructed, however, that it can be dismantled step by step as soon as the market situation permits it. This was promised when the general price freeze was imposed.

In addition to these means of direct intervention, the Yugoslav government has at its disposal a series of other instruments of financial and credit policy that are modified very frequently and that do not deserve detailed discussion at this time. The question of Yugoslavia's possible rapprochement with a market-economic system has less to do with the character of these instruments than with the following considerations:

First, it may be taken for granted that the Yugoslav enterprises, which operate within a specific political system, will react in a typical way to specific economic measures, as has already been illustrated by a few examples. It may therefore be assumed that the instruments of economic policy commonly applied in Western market economies will generate different reactions in Yugoslav economic units. The notion of "means-and-end" mix ought therefore to be generally different than in the West.

Second, the application of the principle of workers' self-management seems to deprive the state of certain guiding instruments: In accordance with the postulate of "de-etatization," the state is supposed substantially to withdraw from economic life. As a result, it can use only the narrow framework of fiscal policy to assure internal economic stability. This raises a serious question as to the future of over-all economic policy, namely: Will over-all policy continue to rely on authoritarian price and distribution controls to offset this limitation? Apart from this question, and apart from the need to improve the tools of monetary and credit policy, Yugoslavia still lacks the means—compatible with its system—for an effective and flexible response to domestic demand.

Income Distribution

The problems of income distribution deserve ever greater attention as the decentralization of the right to dispose of profits continues.

In a system of enterprises managed by workers who are entitled to a considerable share of the profit, the workers should be regarded as collective entrepreneurs. The price of labor is not determined by supply and demand in the labor market, nor is it negotiated between management and labor representatives. As to the over-all economic problems of this system of income distribution, one may recall the discussion of workers' participation (Mitbestimmung) in West Germany. The problem of income distribution in Yugoslavia is, however, not merely economic but social as well. Thus, since the workers' income depends ultimately on the disparities in profitability and market position of the various enterprises, the result is contrary to the fundamental concept of the Yugoslav system, that is, reward depends on competitive performance. This applies also to the disparities in the distribution of wealth, since something approaching income from property might be the final result. How important this problem of income inequality has become emerges from increasingly bitter discussions in Yugoslavia itself. It sounds almost paradoxical to find out that the extent of the social problem arising from the distribution of income is almost as great as in a capitalist market economy. The primary reason for adopting a Socialist economic system—the social problem of an unjust distribution of wealth—is emerging in a new, yet most familiar form.

The Foreign Trade System

Yugoslavia's inclination to experiment is particularly pronounced in the field of foreign economic policy. Its foreign trade system is very complicated and cannot be treated here in detail. The conclusions drawn from a more thorough investigation[13] are summarized below:

The institutions, aims, and tools of foreign economic policy have changed in the course of transforming the Yugoslav economic system. However, it is evident that the liberalization of the foreign economic sector always followed decentralization and liberalization of the domestic economy with a certain time-lag. This may in part be attributed to the legacy of past inefficient economic policy, which was pursued under central planning and with autarkic objectives in mind. The gradual steps toward decentralization and utilization of the market in the domestic economy brought to light disproportions and disequilibria which could not be countered except by a gradual long-term adjustment to conditions on the world market. During the transitional period it was necessary to continue a restrictive foreign-trade policy (which was, however, fundamentally modified in the course of time).

A survey of the development and basic features of foreign economic policy suggests that a clear shift from direct to indirect measures and from quantitative to value-oriented restrictions has taken place. The new system also permits more selective interventions in monetary and foreign exchange matters, which have also become more differentiated and therefore more effective than before. All these changes are the result of domestic economic reform and are essential if Yugoslavia is to be integrated in the international division of labor of the Western world.

The development of a socialist market economy and the need to take part in the international division of labor produced a liberalization of external economic relations. A partial liberalization of commodity trade also called for a gradual elimination of foreign-exchange controls (their complete elimination cannot be expected in the next few years because of the persistent balance-of-payments deficit). For this reason it is paramount for Yugoslavia to continue to diminish the deficit in its balance of trade, especially services, in order to alleviate the very heavy burden on its capital and foreign exchange account. However, it seems that—at least in the present situation—this cannot be achieved with the help of foreign trade measures, alone, such as export promotion, import restrictions, and foreign exchange controls, even though accompanying measures, such as a liberalization of the movement of labor and capital (joint ventures and foreign investments), support this objective. The restoration of domestic economic stability is an essential prerequisite for balance-of-payments equilibrium and for integration with international trade.

The development of the Yugoslav foreign trade system shows that, in decentralizing a Socialist economic system both internally and externally (disregarding the specific case of workers' self-management), tension is bound to arise calling for the application of carefully harmonized instruments of internal and external economic policy. This applies especially to the effects of exchange-rate, trade, and foreign-exchange policy, not only on costs, prices and economic growth but also on the distribution of income as decentralization progresses.

The Yugoslav reforms in the internal and foreign economic fields have already been successful in improving economic cooperation with the Western industrial nations and in creating the preconditions for Yugoslavia's admission to full membership in GATT in 1966.

The elimination of foreign trade monopoly and the direct involvement of Yugoslav enterprises in foreign trade did their part in creating favorable conditions for industrial cooperation with Western firms. Up to the present, the development of this cooperation has had positive effects on the Yugoslav economy and on the structure of mutual commodity exchanges. It may be further expanded, particularly because accumulated long-term experience is a useful guideline.

As the first Socialist country in Eastern Europe to do so in 1967, Yugoslavia offers the possibility of investment in domestic firms to interested foreign parties. Numerous advantages of the Yugoslav economy favor establishing such partnerships, yet—at the same time—frictions will be unavoidable in this field, due, in particular, to differences in the respective property and economic systems, which set limits to the possibilities of international cooperation.[14]

Political Effects of the Reforms

Following the proclamation of workers' self-management as an institutional norm in the Constitution of 1963 and subsequent constitutional amendments, it became increasingly necessary to apply the idea of "self-management" in the field of politics as well. Many communists in Yugoslavia aspire to a socialist social and economic order that is protected from the totalitarian use of power by state and party, and from bureaucratic intrusions on the part of executive organs.[15]

This ideological attitude implies a new role for the communist party. Unlike in other communist countries, the Yugoslav party is not an organization with the power to determine almost everything. The party's leading role is questioned, particularly in the economic sphere. This, however, is not sufficient reason to expect radical changes in the basic political system.

In addition to a growing public discussion of these and similar issues, there are further indications of advancing democratization—greater individual rights and liberties and greater autonomy for the constituent republics. Also, the growing role of the Federal Assembly (Parliament) in political and economic decision-making was reflected in an extension of the Assembly's functions and in the fact that bills introduced by the government are frequently defeated or amended in heated parliamentary debates.

The new Constitution of 1963 prescribed a comprehensive system of constitutional jurisprudence by establishing a Supreme Court. The actual application of the Constitution shows that decisions against state organs are indeed possible when these organs interfere with certain self-management rights and general statutory freedoms of the individual citizens.

The reasons for this development are complex; only some of the most important can be mentioned below:

A younger, more progressive and broad-minded generation is moving up the party leadership ladder. This generation has lived through the development of self-management and is aware of the advantages of this Yugoslav system over the centrally controlled economies and societies in the other countries of Eastern Europe.

Moreover, a number of the younger people have spent extensive periods of study in Western countries, mainly the USA, and also as temporary employees of international organizations. Although remaining communists by conviction, they have clear ideas of the functioning of a modern political system, which they wish to combine with the concept of self-management. Their advance into the important policy-making organs of the party has had a decisive influence on the shaping of political and especially economic relations with the West European countries. Significant in this connection is the continued division of the party into "orthodox" and "progressive" wings. The "orthodox" wing has been unable to develop principles other than those that have already proved harmful in the past. The arguments of the "progressive" reformers seem to have become more convincing, not only among the people at large but also in the party, especially as economic difficulties have increased (partially as a result of the recentralization measures of 1962-63, initiated by the orthodox wing).

Differences of opinion and attitude resulting from historical, regional, and nationalistic tensions are a further important factor influencing economic, cultural, and political life. One special problem that has existed since the inception of the multinational state of Yugoslavia is the considerable economic, historical, and cultural differences among the individual republics and regions. The new nationalism now evident in the party and government—contrary to prewar nationalism—derives substantially from economic problems. This could be perceived in the perennial intra-party disputes over the economic reforms—although economic issues can be used as cover-ups for political and ethnic animosities, as the December 1971 events in Croatia seem to indicate.[16]

The cardinal problem confronting Yugoslavia today is the conflict between the principle of self-management and the political monopoly of the party, which is becoming more pronounced despite the above-mentioned modifications. Chances for permitting a second political party are currently non-existent. Nevertheless, it is important to note that certain ideas are indeed beginning to spill over from the economic to the political sphere, with potentially explosive implications.

Concluding Remarks

The organization of the economic system and the shaping of economic policy have not yet been completed. Nevertheless, the Yugoslav economy—if one disregards the adjective "socialist" as an expression of a particular form of ownership, and despite some still existing centralistic elements—is already closer to the Western market-oriented than to the Eastern command-oriented economies and is actually years ahead of the latter, both theoretically and practically. The gradual removal of direct controls by the state—greater independence for the enterprises and reduced intervention by the party in economic affairs, accompanied by a greater role for the Federal Assembly (Parliament) and the individual republics—is a sign of a fundamental transformation of the economic and social order. Regardless of future developments, it seems safe to assume that, given existing political realities, two extreme possibilities are out of the question in the foreseeable future: a return to a centrally administered economy of the Soviet type, on the one hand, and the adoption of a capitalist economic order relying on private ownership of capital, on the other.

Notes

1. A comprehensive and systematic description of the Yugoslav economic system is contained *inter alia* in P. Dobias, "Das jugoslawische Wirtschaftssystem: Entwicklung und Wirkungsweise" (The Yugoslav Economic System: Development and Method of Operation), *Kieler Studien*, no. 100, Kiel, 1969; S. Pejovich, *The Market-Planned Economy of Yugoslavia* (Minneapolis, 1966); H. Schleicher, *Das System der betrieblichen Selbstverwaltung in Jugoslawien* (The Workers' Self-Management System in Yugoslavia) (Berlin, 1961); and International Labour Office, *Die Arbeiterselbstverwaltung in den Betrieben Jugoslawiens* (Workers' Self-Management in Yugoslav Enterprises), Geneva, 1962. It is noteworthy that a comprehensive and thorough analysis of the Yugoslav economic system has yet to appear in Yugoslavia.

2. The 1950 Law in *Sluzbeni List FNRJ* (Official Gazette), no. 43, 1950. The 1952 Law, ibid., no. 17, 1952.

3. Cf. R. Bicanic, "The Economics of Socialism in a Developed Country," *Foreign Affairs*, vol. 44, no. 4, 1966.

4. The pertinent legislation is in *Sluzbeni List*, no. 33 ff., 1965.

5. Cf. L.A.D. Dellin, "Agriculture and the Peasant," in Stephen Fischer-Galati, ed., *Eastern Europe in the Sixties* (New York: Praeger, 1963), pp. 76-80.

6. Appropriate provisions in *Sluzbeni List*, nos. 51 and 52, 1953.

7. Ibid., no. 33, 1965.

8. See Dobias, op. cit., p. 1 ff.; D. Meier, *Besteuerung und Finanzierung der jugoslawischen Industrieunternehmungen im Vergleich mit deutschen Aktiengesellschaften* (Taxation and Funding of Yugoslav Industrial Enterprises: A Comparison with German Joint-Stock Companies), (unpublished doctoral dissertation, Munich University), p. 63 ff.

9. Cf. Harry Schleicher, op. cit., supra and Jiri Kolaja, *Workers Councils: The Yugoslav Experience* (New York: Praeger, 1966).

10. See G. Leman, *Stellung und Aufgaben der oekonomischen Einheiten in den jugoslawischen Unternehmungen* (The Role of Economic Units in Yugoslav Enterprises) (Berlin, 1967).

11. The corresponding legal provisions are in *Sluzbeni List*, no. 35, 1965.

12. Banking Act in *Sluzbeni List*, no. 12, 1965.

13. See J. Hawlowitsch, "Jugoslawien" (Yugoslavia), in J. Meier and J. Hawlowitsch, eds., *Die Aussenwirtschaft Suedosteuropas* (Southeastern Europe's Foreign Commerce) (Cologne, 1960).

14. The foreign investment legislation passed in 1967 was subsequently amended in 1971 so as to permit expatriation of all foreign earnings and paid-in capital, which was one of the major obstacles for successful cooperation (cf. *Sluzbeni List*, no. 31, July 19, 1967 and no. 29, July 28, 1971). It should also be mentioned that foreign aid and loans to Yugoslavia, mainly from the United States and amounting to about seven billion dollars over the last twenty-five years, were very crucial for the country's economy (cf. *The Wall Street Journal*, June 4, 1971).

15. See the author's "Die Sozialistische Foederative Republik Jugoslawien" (The Socialist Federative Republic of Yugoslavia) in A. Domes, ed., *Osteuropa und die Hoffnung auf Freiheit* (Eastern Europe and the Hope for Freedom), Cologne, 1967, p. 216 ff.

16. As a result of these events, the party leadership was re-centralized but continued economic reform remained a professed goal (see the "Action Program" of the Second Party Conference in *Borba*, Jan. 29, 1972).

9 Conclusion: Is There a Congruence

Karl C. Thalheim

I

The general theme of our symposium—"Congruence of the Economic Systems?"—is punctuated with a question mark, which seems amply justified after the presentation of the papers. The term congruence, taken literally, goes further than the word convergence, which is the commonly used term in this connection. Congruence means complete overlapping, that is, a development process whereby systems that were originally quite different eventually overlap completely or overlap at least in their essential points.

It is well known that for almost ten years this problem of systems convergence has been the subject of heated discussions among economists and, even more so, in the daily and periodical press. As a rule, economists are generally more careful in addressing themselves to this question than are many journalists.

Evidently what is meant by the interrogative is at least a search for an answer: are the economic systems getting closer to one another— are they converging to the point of congruence as a result of the changes taking place in the various countries under discussion?

It is a commonplace that changes are continually taking place in all economic systems of the world. Never in history was there an economic system that, once conceived and realized, continued unchanged over a long period of time. Economic systems cannot be compared with a mass shaped once and for all in an inflexible mold. On the contrary, they are living forms on the move. We are confronted today with precisely such movement, both in the East and in the West, to use the conventional terms.

In this process of changing economic systems, all serious scholars speak of changes affecting both sides, East as well as West, and not only of one of the systems or one category of systems moving exclusively in the direction of the other. Communism does not become capitalism. Yet capitalism does not become communism either, in spite of the fact that even today Soviet ideology defends a special kind of a one-sided convergence theory, according to which the capitalist economic system must develop in the direction of socialism and communism. Perhaps you remember the sentence contained in the 1961 Soviet party Program: "Communism is the bright future of all mankind." In other words, there is no ultimate development other than in the direction of communism.

If one wanted to do full justice to the topic, one would investigate the changes that are taking place in the economic systems of the West and try answering the question: Are changes under way in the West that indicate a rapprochement with the systems of the East? I am sure that to attempt to answer this would be over-ambitious within the framework of a paper designed to summarize the findings of our presentations, because they concentrate on reform movements in the East only. From time to time, I shall, however, try to throw some light on the development process in the West. In general, though, I would like to stay within the assigned theme of the symposium: Do the changes that have taken place and continue to take place in the economic systems of the East mean that they are converging with the economic systems of the West—which would presuppose a congruence among themselves?

Two groups say yes: there is, first, the group of super-optimists in the West, those convinced of the advantages of the Western systems who argue that the Western economic order is bound to prevail sooner or later all over the world. They argue, in other words, that the logic of things must unfailingly lead to the establishment of a market economy everywhere, perhaps even a free-enterprise market economy. Popularly, this thesis is expounded by the press and the other mass media under captions such as "Red Profits," suggesting that communist systems are gradually transforming themselves into capitalistic systems.

At the opposite end is found the group of "orthodox" communists who are equally convinced that all reforms in Socialist countries mean a return to capitalism. Professor Sik himself is one of the men whom the orthodox communists branded as a prophet of the restoration of capitalism.

To my mind both sides are mistaken. I have already mentioned that most economists are much more careful in their judgment than is the press, that their views are often over-simplified by their non-scholarly interpreters. Such was the case with the scholarly article on the convergence thesis by the Dutch economist Tinbergen, winner of the new Nobel Prize for Economics.[1] This article was interpreted quite carelessly in the public information media.

In attempting to draw conclusions from the papers presented here, which gave us such a clear picture of the successful and unsuccessful reforms in communist Europe, the most important thing is that a uniform picture fails to emerge. If we wish to answer the question posed by my topic, it is necessary to make three differentiations: *First*, we must differentiate among the kinds of reforms in the individual countries. Thus, considering Professor Nove's paper on the Soviet Union, on the one hand, and that by Professor Hawlowitsch on Yugoslavia, on the other, it becomes obvious that these two countries have introduced reforms that are quite different in form, objective, and degree of effectiveness.

The *second* differentiation concerns the dissimilarity between certain components of the systems, which will be detailed later on. By components or elements of the system we mean, first of all, the elements of the economic system. The *third* aspect of differentiation involves elements making up the entire life of society, of which the economy is only one. It was fortunate that this interrelationship was stressed in the papers and discussions; the different interpretations reveal how important this problem is, and how difficult it is to answer. This third aspect, then, concerns the relationship between the economic order, the political order, and the social order. The question is whether and to what extent a uniform trend of development is present in these three realms of human life. Are mutual interlockings inevitable, or is it possible for these three realms to develop independently of one another?

The papers and discussions were especially concerned with the question as to whether and to what degree the political order and the economic order are directly related, perhaps even dependent on each other in a cause-and-effect sequence. Let me recall the thought of an economist whom I regard highly, and to whom I owe much of my intellectual development, Walter Eucken, who spoke of an "interdependence of the orders."[2] This formulation points to the mutual interdependence of these areas of human life. It will, of course, be impossible to determine a clear causal relationship; but there is no doubt that the various realms of life influence each other, perhaps in the sense that they drive one another forward.

The differences among the various countries were made very clear in our papers. One country was not covered, the German Democratic Republic, and I would like to draw a sketch of it, not because it is my major subject of teaching and research,[3] but because it is not without interest in the present context—it was the first of the Socialist countries to introduce genuine economic reforms. I have stressed elsewhere, both orally and in writing,[4] that to my mind many Western misinterpretations arise because no proper distinction is made between reform stages such as discussion of reforms, experimentation, and actual reforms that affect the system as a whole. In many cases one confuses mere discussions, for example in *Pravda*, with reality. In Professor Dellin's paper on Bulgaria, we were shown how important it is to distinguish between reform blueprint and reform implementation.

The German Democratic Republic was indeed the first Socialist country to introduce a major economic reform; this so-called "new system of planning and management" was initiated in the summer of 1963. Personally, I am of the opinion that the German Democratic Republic was consciously selected by the USSR as a kind of a guinea-pig country for such reforms, because the GDR was the most advanced economy in the Soviet bloc and could have indicated what impact reform might have on the USSR itself.

For two or three years the German Democratic Republic continued to act as a pace-setter for reforms, but then it lost this leading role to other countries. Leaving Yugoslavia aside, the reforms in Hungary and those in Czechoslovakia before the Soviet intervention in August 1968 went considerably further than the reforms in East Germany, where changes in the economic sphere would have affected the political order—something that the regime was not prepared to tolerate.

II

In attempting to investigate the structure of the European Socialist countries on the basis of economic reforms, three different types become distinguishable: the "conservative," the "compromising," and the "progressive" types.

—The conservatives cling to the old rigid centralized system of planning and management as a matter of principle and merely try to make the system more efficient by employing better technical methods. Hence the emphasis on giant computers, etc., in the Soviet Union, which was mentioned by Professor Sik. One question remaining to be answered in this context is: Are those who defend such methods, that is, the mathematical methods and the automation of planning, necessarily identical with economic centralists? I do not think that this question can definitely be answered in the affirmative, for such methods may also be employed in carrying out different kinds of reforms; yet it is now mostly the conservatives who speak of these methods.

At this moment no true conservatives are in power in any one of the Socialist countries, except perhaps in Albania, but it is my impression, confirmed in most of the presented papers, that conservative groups of varying strength do exist in practically all of the Socialist states, and that it is not altogether impossible that they may return to power some time in the future.

—The second group is composed of what I call the compromisers. It includes all the member-states of the Council for Mutual Economic Assistance (Comecon) except Hungary and—until a short time ago— Czechoslovakia. I am afraid that today Czechoslovakia no longer belongs to this group. The compromisers are those who, although upholding the principle of central planning and management, have realized the shortcomings of the system and are consequently trying to incorporate "quasi-market" elements in it. These elements include: substituting for the familiar "deduction from profits" interest-like contributions by the enterprises for the use of real or money capital; using the actual sales volume as a measure of performance in place of gross output; applying a price policy that, although not intending to let prices reflect relative scarcities, tries to bring them closer to production costs; a partial transfer of decision-making from the center to the enterprise, whereby one of its variants is becoming more important all the time, namely the transfer of decision-making to "socialist trusts" (such as the "VVB's" in the German Democratic Republic). In this connection, an important question arises that is difficult, even impossible, to answer at this time: Is such a compromise workable in the long run; will it, or will it not, resolve difficulties? It must be stated at least tentatively that the results of the trust system in the German Democratic Republic are not unfavorable so far, and that the obvious stagnation there in the early 1960s has been overcome. I do not believe that the overcoming of stagnation is entirely attributable to the new economic system, but the economic reform certainly did play a role. It is doubtful, however, whether these results can be generalized and applied to other countries. For this reason, it will be most important to follow East German developments very closely in the next few years.

—The third group, the "progressive" countries, is in favor of a "socialist market economy." This phenomenon has been treated and explained in the various papers. An essential feature of the socialist market economy is the preservation of socialist property, with possible exceptions in relatively unimportant sectors. However, the preservation of socialist property is countered by the abandonment of centralized planning, which is to be converted into "structural planning," whatever that may mean; and guidance functions are to be transferred to the market mechanism or, consequently, to the price mechanism.

This group of "progressive" countries comprises two distinct sub-groups: Yugoslavia, as a special example of a "socialist market economy" with workers' self–management in the enterprises, on the one hand, and Hungary as well as the Czechoslovak reformers, whose plans were so convincingly described by Professor Sik, on the other. We learned from Mr. Sik that the workers' councils in Czechoslovakia were to be different from workers' self-management in Yugoslavia. And in Hungary there is no intention whatever to introduce workers' self-management of the Yugoslav type.

III

I have divided these countries into three groups in order to be able to answer the question implied in the topic of my paper. It is plain to see that the three groups of countries are very dissimilar, as far as the degree of convergence and congruence with non-communist countries is concerned. Convergence in the real sense of the term seems to be entirely absent in the "conservative" group. This applies not only to the economic system but also to the political and the social orders of these countries, where the situation has not appreciably changed for quite some time. The big problem for the future, which is constantly discussed in scholarly literature, is whether this system can cope with a modern industrial society in the long run. Are not serious difficulties bound to arise in a modern society, difficulties that cannot possibly be overcome by a centralized system with a party monopoly?

A certain degree of congruence or convergence can be found among what I called the "compromising" countries, because these countries admit certain elements of the market economy. It is precisely this phenomenon that has led some Western observers to assume that genuine convergence is under way. However, such does not seem to be the case. To my mind, what is happening in this group cannot yet be considered as convergence in the true sense of the term, for the quality of market elements necessarily changes when they are introduced in a centrally-controlled Socialist system. They assume a character which is quite different from what they have in a market economy.

Thus, although greater importance is now being attached to enterprise profit in compromising countries than was the case under the old system, the nature and the quality of this type of profit are still different from what they are in a market economy. This is so because, as long as the central plan is considered the most important device for directing and controlling the economy, the enterprises will be unable to gear their production plan to anticipated profit, or at most they will be able to do so only in those areas in which the plan permits them some freedom of action. Of course, such areas do exist, but they are limited in scope and importance. As a result, profit cannot perform its decisive functions as it does in market economies, even though it bears the same name and, in a formal and superficial sense, is supposed to be something similar or even identical to its Western counterpart.

On the other hand, if one considers the direction in which the "socialist market" economics are moving, and the fact that in the Western economies changes are taking place that tend to diminish the old sharp distinctions between the two systems, one may speak in terms of a rather significant degree of rapprochement. To mention just a few examples: even in market-oriented economies certain capital goods are collectively owned or controlled in various shapes or forms; they may be state-owned, owned by local authority, or owned by foundations, and the like. Moreover, government intervention in most Western countries is much more significant today than was or should be the case in truly "free-market" economies; indeed, is there anywhere a "free-market" economy today? Finally, some prices in the West are influenced in one form or another by forces outside the market; surely nobody will maintain that the present agricultural market systems in the European Common Market member states or in the United States reflect the principles of a market economy.

Thus, changes have been under way in the West that also tend to reduce differences between the systems. If the defenders of what is called market socialism visualize a genuine transition of their economies from central planning and control to the market as the guiding force, and if the basic decision-making power is transferred from the central authority to the management of the enterprises, then a far-reaching rapprochement would obviously be taking place on the other side as well.

Once the process of transferring decision-making to the level of the individual enterprise is implemented, a further rapprochement of the goals of the different economies must necessarily result; the enterprises in a socialist market economy will also begin to seek profit and will try to find out what sort of output and supply will yield the highest gain. Aside from monopolistic, oligopolistic, or other extreme market structures, this will only be possible if the enterprises are in a position to satisfy existing demand or a demand they may succeed in creating. Thus, a convergence of objectives must also take place, especially in the Western market-oriented economies the aims of economic activity are no longer determined exclusively by the consumer, as ideally imagined in the textbooks of fifty years ago. Considering that in all Western countries a large proportion of the national income is generated by the government budget and thus not determined by the consumer, one can see that very significant changes have occurred in the West as well.

A prerequisite for decentralization of decision-making is, naturally, that managers should be able to rely on information derived from the market. This was made sufficiently clear in the various papers. Professor Sik, in particular, emphasized that this signaling by the market of the relative scarcities of goods can be obtained solely through prices reflecting real market forces. I fully agree with Professor Sik's position, because I am unable to visualize how a market might be simulated by whatever mathematical-technological aids; after all, a market has to deal with not only hundreds but several thousands or even millions of goods and prices.

Furthermore, "market socialism" means the existence of competition, including price competition, as is the case with any other market-oriented economy. Certainly there are many other forms of competition, but a market economy without price competition is a *non sequitur*. It is interesting to note in this connection that the same problems that currently exist in Western market economies arise in the minds of adherents of a socialist market—the problems of monopoly. I have in mind the various Western laws against restraints of trade, on the one hand, and Professor Sik's elaborations, on the other, as to how the monopolistic positions of single enterprises or groups of enterprises created by the old system might be eliminated by a socialist market economy of the sort that the reformers had planned to introduce in Czechoslovakia. The problems in both cases are very similar.

The role that foreign economic relations should play in a socialist market economy seems to be similar to that played in Western market-oriented economies, as we so clearly see from the Conference papers. The complete isolation of the domestic from the world market was an integral element of the Stalinist system in the communist economies. We were told by first-hand witnesses of the dire consequences of this isolation. It is characteristic of all attempts to establish a socialist market economy that the reformers intended to tear down the rigid wall protecting the domestic from the foreign markets. This razing of barriers is an essential prerequisite for success and means, for example, that prices obtained for exports must immediately affect the exporting enterprises, and that subsidies compensating losses would no longer be paid by the state.

Let me add that similar trends may also be observed among the group of "compromiser" states. In the German Democratic Republic, for instance, they are trying to let foreign trade prices have a direct effect on the enterprises concerned. However, this attempt seems to be much more difficult within the framework of the East German system than in a true socialist market economy.

IV

After all is said and done, a great difference continues to exist between socialist market economies and Western market economies where the ownership of the means of production is concerned. On this point I do not quite agree with the author of the paper on Yugoslavia, in whose opinion ownership is an exclusively juridical rather than an economic category. To my own mind, the problem of ownership is economic to the extent that it is closely connected with opportunities for action in matters economic. Independent economic action is difficult if at all possible to imagine without private ownership of the means of production.

It is not my intention to argue which is the "better" system, the system of private ownership or that of socialist ownership. I merely wish to emphasize that a really crucial difference between the two does exist; it was mentioned previously that this difference has been reduced by changes in the Western economies, and that the ideas and intentions of "market socialism" are also likely to diminish it further. Professor Sik, for example, found it possible and even desirable for private business activity in crafts and services to operate within a socialist system. In Yugoslavia, most farming is done by private owners, while the Czechoslovak reformers—according to Sik—had been in favor of retaining collective farming.

In spite of similarities between and within the Socialist and Western systems, I am prone to deny, at least for the time being, the existence of a substantive congruence or convergence as we have defined it. I shall not speculate about long-term possibilities: nobody knows what the world may look like a hundred years from now; everything is possible. But as to the present, one must admit that even a "socialist market economy" reaches a point where rapprochement of the economic systems ends. This point or "sound barrier" is notably the ownership of the means of production—the possibility of an independent economic existence and business activity, or the lack of it.

At this point one should emphasize that it is important for economists to discuss not only the general framework of the various economic systems but also to go into details that, while often tricky, sometimes provide very positive lessons. For example, one should also pose and explore the following question, which was suggested by the paper on Yugoslavia: Is there a difference between the position of a corporation manager in a capitalist country and that of an enterprise manager in a socialist market economy? We would probably agree that the position of a manager of a state-owned enterprise in the Soviet Union today is different from the position of a manager of a corporation in a capitalistic state. However, would these differences tend to disappear in a "socialist market economy," or would they not? These are questions that have not yet been thoroughly examined. To give a different example: What will be the role of a capital market in a socialist market economy if the principle is upheld that the only permissible income is labor income? How can a capital market be organized under these circumstances? What would its functions be as compared with those of a capital market in a capitalist country? What would be the role of interest? In what way might the interest rate act as a regulator of economic activity in a socialist market economy? All these questions appear to be very important, yet many of them have been neglected by Western economists, because—it seems—they do not fit fully into the formulae used in present-day economics. As a result, they are not considered important enough by some of our fellow-economists.

V

Finally, let us ask a basic question: What is the relationship between the economy and the other areas of social life and, in particular, between the economic and the political order? Several of the preceding papers called attention to forces that have inhibited or are still inhibiting the economic reforms. If I am right, such obstacles fit into three groups:

First of all, there is the ideological commitment of the majority of party leaderships in communist countries—commitment not only to "Marxism" generally, but to the specific Soviet-brand of Marxism which maintains, among other things, that the market and socialism are utterly incompatible. This is a notion still held by many present-day communist leaders. I would call this the ideological obstacle.

The second obstacle—which I am sure Professor Sik would confirm from the experience of Czechoslovakia—is that some managers of nationalized enterprises are not at all eager to carry out the reforms.

They do not feel equal to the demands of a socialist market economy and to the decision-making power expected of them within the framework of such an economy, simply because they lack the background, education, and mental attitudes required of them.

The third obstacle—stressed with great force here—is the fear among the leadership that the party might lose its power monopoly. I think we all agree that many communist party leaders considered this the crux which made them decide to refrain from really meaningful reforms. A related question arises that I feel unprepared to resolve as an economist, but that is important to the political sociologist: Why are the attitudes of the leaderships so different in the individual countries? Why is the leadership of the Yugoslav community party, for example, prepared to make much greater concessions, or why is the communist leadership in Hungary ready to go much farther than, for instance, the leadership of the German Democratic Republic?

As previously mentioned, I do not believe that the relationship between the political and the economic order can be viewed simply as a cause-and-effect relationship—neither in the sense that a certain economic order necessarily creates a specific political order, nor in the sense that a given political order results inevitably in a specific economic order. However, I submit that certain political preconditions must be created if a given economic order is to be made possible.

To give an opposite example: a free-market economy is basically incompatible within a totalitarian state. And, vice-versa, I believe that central planning of the Stalinist type is also unthinkable in a parliamentary democracy. Thus, to my mind, certain political preconditions must indeed exist, particularly in order to implement economic reforms of the "progressive type." Therefore, the distinction between "progressive" reforms and reforms of a more careful, "compromising" nature is very important in this regard.

Reforms of the "compromising" type can also be carried out in a centralized political system where the Party holds a monopoly of power. However, experience seems to show that progressive reforms cannot be realized in such a political system, inasmuch as they require that the party leadership be prepared to make concessions restricting its power monopoly. Even the transfer of managerial decision-making from the center down to the level of the enterprise management means restricting the party's power.

A further pertinent question was alluded to in the discussions, but was not—as it perhaps could not be—answered in full: If, for reasons of economic necessity, a country is induced or forced to initiate progressive economic reforms, will these reforms necessarily lead to changes in the political order, or even in the social order and the structure of society? Some considerations seem to speak in favor of this assumption, yet only in the long run: chain reactions, possibly of long duration, are not at all impossible. This applies especially to the problem of the party's power monopoly.

The question of restricting the political power of the party leadership seems to me of very great importance for future developments. In this connection I am a bit skeptical about the potential role of the "technocrats," who seem to be very highly rated by many Western authors. Occasionally one even hears that the technocrats, who are pressing for the top and will eventually assume the leadership, will—to oversimplify—pursue different policies. I am not sure whether these technocrats are sufficiently interested in politics to risk a battle for political power. Let me refer to the biography of a typical technocrat in a totalitarian state, namely Herr Speer under Hitler, published recently.[5] Undoubtedly, Speer was a technocrat of the highest order, but he did not at all try to influence the totalitarian system of the Brown Dictator; on the contrary, he put his abilities at the service of that system.

Therefore, I am still unable to see why the rise of the technocrats, who undoubtedly are an important part of a modern industrial society, is supposed to cause a change in the political structure; it seems questionable, and even dangerous, to place great hopes on this kind of reasoning. The decisive question seems to be whether the communist leaderships themselves will move in the direction of allowing autonomous social forces to come to the fore; and I mean social forces which are not represented by the party machine or the state apparatus.

In this connection, the altered circumstances of the trade unions in countries carrying out progressive reforms—which was confirmed in several of the Conference papers—seems to me a matter of much importance. We all know that under the old system the trade unions had no autonomous power, that they were—to use the famous comparison by Lenin—mere transmission belts between the party and the working masses. However, in Yugoslavia and to a certain degree in Hungary, the trade unions have begun claiming and gaining a role as autonomous forces in society, and, according to the plans of the Czechoslovak reformers, the same development would have taken place in their country as well. (Only in that case would economic reforms have produced changes in the social order.) This is the area upon which we may pin our hopes.

In conclusion, I do not think that, although real congruence and convergence do not exist, one should necessarily predict a continuing "cold war." In fact, world history is full of examples of "hot wars" between countries with the same economic, political, and social orders. I do not see why complete convergence, even if it were possible or desirable, would necessarily prevent conflicts among nations. Nor do I believe that complete convergence is a necessary prerequisite of cooperation between states with different economic and social orders.

Notes

1. Jan Tinbergen, "Do Communist and Free Economies Show a Converging Pattern?," in *Soviet Studies*, vol. 7, April 1961.

2. Walter Eucken, *Grundsaetze der Wirtschaftspolitik* (Principles of Economic Policy) (Tüebingen, 1960, third edition).

3. Cf. my *Die Wirtschaft der Sowjetzone in Krise und Umbau* (The Economy of the Soviet Zone in Crisis and Reconstruction) (Berlin, 1964); the blueprint in *Gesetzblatt der DDR* (Legal Gazette of the GDR), No. 64, 1963.

4. Cf. my "Liberalisierungstendenzen im Ostblock?" (Liberalization Tendencies in the Eastern Bloc?), in B. Gleize, K.C. Thalheim, K.P. Hensel and R. Meimberg, *Der Osten auf dem Wege zur Marktwirtschaft* (The East on the Road to a Market Economy) (Berlin, 1967).

5. Albert Speer, *Inside the Third Reich: Memoirs* (New York, 1970).

10 Epilogue

L. A. D. Dellin

I

The main purpose of this epilogue is not to repeat or summarize what has been said by the previous authors but to consider some unfinished business and the tasks that lay ahead, as discerned in the perceptive presentations and discussions of this symposium. In other words, what follows will be as much an epilogue of the work done as a prologue for future effort.

The thrust of the symposium has been on economic reforms in the general sense and on the domestic scene of individual countries. What remained beyond the scope of the conference—and should now be supplemented—were country-by-country comparisons as to reform plans and their implementation, trends of reforms, and interactions between domestic economies and international trade—although there were sporadic references to them. Moreover, the expanded scope of inquiry should also stimulate the work on improved analytical models which would permit more meaningful comparisons among Communist (Socialist) systems or cultures.

All these are areas that deserve additional attention not only as far as their problem-solving is concerned but also in order to give due recognition to the scholarly work already done in these fields; this should explain the use of many source references in the footnotes below, so as to remedy for the lack of a separate bibliographical section (sources quoted are generally from the mid-1960s onward).

II

In order to be able to make a proper assessment of the current state of economic reform in communist Europe, one must ask the question: *What, if any, are the differences between reform proposals, officially-approved reform blueprints, and reform implementation?* (Experimentation with some features of the reform, wherever applicable, could be treated separately or as part of the implementation phase.)

Although there are many, often insuperable, difficulties in clearly identifying these phases—especially the exact degree of implementation—a satisfactory answer to this question should not be hard to find once it is agreed that discrepancies—great or small—definitely exist. But the inclination to neglect the differences between proposals, blueprints, and implementation is too prevalent in the West. Thus, many of us were either (understandably) impressed by the opening of a Pandora's Box in communist Europe after Stalin's death, when completely unexpected criticism of the existing system and proposals for reforming it began saturating us to the point that it became very difficult if at all possible to distinguish word from deed; or else we were inclined—in our belief that things have got to change sooner or later—to see change before it took place, if indeed it ever took place.

It therefore comes as a salutary reminder, if not as a surprise, when Nove characterizes the Soviet case as "the reform that never was," or when—so I was told—the history of economic reforms in Bulgaria is compared to a "tempest in a teapot." And need one recall the outcome of reform in Czechoslovakia?[1]

These, among others, were countries in which debate about the need and extent of economic reforms had raged, especially among economists, since the death of Stalin and most openly after Liberman was officially allowed to present his proposals as a basis for discussion, which gave the "green light" to the rest of the bloc as well.[2]

But the economists—from Novozhilov and Kantorovich to Birman and Lisichkin, from Kornai and Kunin to Brus and Sik, just to mention a few—were not to see the core of their more or less wide-ranging proposals adopted by the regimes. The official blueprints were invariably a "conservative" and in some cases an unrecognizable version of their daring schemes.[3]

Even in a country like Czechoslovakia, where Ota Sik was able to assume governmental responsibility and was backed in his efforts by the new Dubcek regime, the difficulties in even partially implementing the reforms proved staggering, last but not least because of the opposition of vested interests. Finally, as domestic resistance to the reforms weakened, Moscow saw to it that they were cut short of realization.[4]

In countries considered as cautious reformers, such as the Soviet Union or Bulgaria, the official blueprints have after considerable delay in application been declared "almost" implemented, yet in practice the centralized planning system has not been changed to any meaningful degree; on the contrary, a reversal toward the traditional pattern of command economy has been openly acknowledged.[5] Poland, after its many ups and downs, seems to be resuming its road to reform under Gierek, but its program is a long-term proposition with many *caveats.*[6] East Germany, the first country to decide on a reform blueprint (in 1963), seems to have stalled.[7] Rumania and Albania are uninterested in any substantive reforms and are instead, improving the command system.[8]

Hungary, which—as of now—has developed the most advanced blueprint within the bloc, and which also leads the bloc with nearly five years of reform implementation, is experiencing difficulties and making it clear that full application will take a long time.[9] Even Yugoslavia, which in 1965 was already an economy quite different from those of the rest of the Eastern states, is behind schedule on several goals of its new post-1965 reforms and has suffered reversals— such as the price freeze. But its unswerving reform commitment is backed with greater credibility than others would inspire and has greater objective chances of success.[10]

As an answer to this first question, it would appear therefore that (a) a gap exists between official reform blueprints and their actual implementation in all of the European communist states; (b) the gap is even greater between unofficial proposals and official plans; (c) even in those cases where lip service is paid to the blueprint, or to the need for reform, delays in total implementation have usually been officially acknowledged, and often the alleged reformed system bears little resemblance to the original blueprint; and (d) wherever serious intent to apply the reform blueprint is evident, the target dates are for all practical purposes indeterminate. In summary, there are discrepancies between goals and reality that should always be kept in mind in current and future research.

The direction of the economic reforms—a logical follow-up question—is less clear. However, with some exceptions, the trend since 1968 has been toward stagnation and even toward a reversal. In any case the history of economic reform has been cyclical in nature, with some steps forward and some backward.[11] It is true that the movement, on the average and if compared with the Stalinist era, has been forward (as if it could have been otherwise), and that in the long run everything is possible. But the most recent past warns us not to assume continued let alone "inevitable," progress, especially since imposed returns to more rigid patterns are always possible—and likely—in a communist system. In fact, 1972 looks hardly better than 1968, as Czechoslovakia, the Soviet Union, Bulgaria and to some extent East Germany, Rumania, and Albania, can be viewed either as "reverses" or "laggards." This leaves Yugoslavia, Hungary, and possibly Poland to carry on. Yet while Yugoslavia alone remains beyond immediate Soviet reach, Hungary and Poland are very much within the sphere of Soviet power. And the current Soviet mood seems less than favorable to reform, especially to the more ambitious reform that Hungary has embarked upon.[12]

Thus, when disregarding internal factors, it seems that any meaningful economic reform[13] must still meet with the approval of Moscow, which keeps a vigilant eye out for the political implications of economic reforms.[14] If there is no enlightened leadership in the Soviet Union—as currently seems to be the case—economic reform in Eastern Europe is hardly going to bear the desired fruit, at least not in the foreseeable future.[15]

III

This leads us to the second question, i.e., *the impact of international economic relations upon internal developments, including economic reform, and vice versa.*[16] The days of autarky—if ever there were such days—are over and the states of Eastern Europe, unlike the Soviet giant, have always depended on foreign trade to a considerable degree.[17]

Dividing the subject into intra-bloc (Comecon) and extra-bloc (East-West) economic relations, it is obvious that the former have been much more important than the latter: despite the reopening of trade with the West since Stalin's death and a continued and rapid increase of East-West Trade, there has been a renewed reliance on intra-bloc trade, particularly since 1968. The emphasis is now on Comecon economic integration, as evidenced by the recently approved "Complex Program" of 1971, which calls for improved methods of trade and for joint ventures in many fields—from planning to science and technology.[18]

Regardless of the evaluation of this Program blueprint (to be implemented in 15 to 20 years), it seems that even if the Comecon integration were to be genuine and democratic, it can hardly produce meaningful changes before resolving the basic dilemma of how to proceed with intra-bloc specialization if individual member-countries follow different roads of domestic economic reform, and also what economic criteria to use in order to assess the eventual gains and losses resulting from such an integration. Should, however, integration *à la russe* be the choice—as it was, after the intervention in

Czechoslovakia and the Soviet slow-down of economic reforms and as it seems to be the case now—it would suggest a Soviet preference for "congruence" and hegemony and would carry serious political as well as economic implications.[19] Rumania's opposition to such an integration is the most obvious.[20] But other countries, particularly Hungary, also tend to see in it a threat, at least to their domestic economic reforms. Officially, of course, Hungary is all in favor of integration, but on terms that thinly veil a basic repudiation of the Soviet blueprint. How otherwise could one interpret Hungary's official "enthusiasm" for Comecon integration, on the one hand, and its insistence on prior "necessary reforms," on the other— reforms that call for free and multilateral trade and settlement of accounts, the reliance on flexible prices and the introduction of a convertible currency?[21] But such a Comecon reform *à la hongroise* is hardly palatable to Moscow, as it runs counter to the current goals and interests of the Soviet Union.[22]

The difficulties of integration or "cooperation" of a purely economic nature are also numerous. One need only mention some of the major ones, such as: arbitrary and inflexible pricing; the lack of convertibility of currency and goods; basic factor immobility across national frontiers; or the substantial continuation of bilateral trade (as befits countries with centrally-planned and state-directed foreign trade) in order to realize the enormity of the task of integration, even if political considerations were completely disregarded.[23]

But if Comecon were to be shaped in accordance with Soviet wishes, a central question arises: How is the "communist world market" to keep abreast of modernization, let alone "catch up with and surpass the West," if it is to aim inward, without participating in the international ("socialist" as well as "capitalist") division of labor?

Here trade with the West becomes important, if not crucial. As we know, a major motivation for opening up and stepping up this trade was the realization in the communist states that the "technological gap" between them and the West was bound to widen unless Western technology, in the broadest sense of the word, was made available to them. Especially the smaller, foreign trade-dependent countries of Eastern Europe saw impelling economic as well as political benefits in expanded trade, particularly with their once traditional West European partners, most notably the German Federal Republic.

The interrelationship between the degree of economic reform in the individual Eastern countries and the degree of their involvement in trade with the West seems most obvious in the case of Yugoslavia and within Comecon, of Hungary. But, although factors apart from economic reform may be encouraging expanded trade with the West, as is the case with Rumania and the German Democratic Republic, or even with "reform laggards" such as the Soviet Union or Bulgaria, it seems clear that meaningful, longer-term, involvement in such trade requires "sacrifices" by the Eastern partners, one of which is broad compliance with the rules of the "foreign-trade game." In other words, expanded trade with the West tends to generate pressures for change in the East, primarily in the field of economics, but possibly in that of politics as well.[24]

It is understandable then why many Communist regimes, primarily the leading power of the bloc, the Soviet Union, are trying to resist these pressures, and why, conversely, Western countries have changed some of their rigid attitudes, policies, and laws in the hope of influencing their Eastern partners.[25] However, the economic obstacles to substantive expansion are well known: the inability of the Comecon states to offer much in the way of attractive merchandise, while their appetite for sophisticated technology from the West is enormous; ensuing trade imbalances that cannot be covered due to a lack of foreign exchange; the need for extraordinary Western credits or Western acceptance of undesirable imports from the East; and the still typical features of the Soviet-type economies to the extent that they still practice foreign trade monopoly, centralizing planning, bilateralism, and non-convertibility, to mention just a few.[26] The newer form of cooperation[27] involving joint production or marketing between Eastern and Western firms tends to accommodate the Eastern partners, because, for example, the swapping of technological processes for future production amounts to a long-term barter, but precisely because of these barter elements, this sort of cooperation does not portend well, since Western firms are not too prone to guarantee long-term sales of the jointly produced items. Even Yugoslavia—which is a case and almost a world apart—would have to accommodate foreign investors much more convincingly than it has until now.[28]

Thus, trade with the West entails "costs" or "penalties," i.e., changing old ways, which few Eastern countries are willing or permitted to do, at least at this time. It is also symptomatic that reforms in the foreign trade field have been trailing reforms in other economic areas. With Czechoslovakia almost out of the picture, Yugoslavia is followed at a great distance by Hungary; Poland, as well as Rumania, although members of GATT, do not seem to be willing to pay the "price" that goes with the "privilege" of trading with the West.

In sum, the prospects for expanded East-West trade are mixed and were dimmed by the Soviet intervention in Czechoslovakia. Since then, Soviet pressures for greater economic integration within Comecon have also meant pressures on the smaller Eastern states for containing contacts with the West, although the Soviets have not felt bound by the same rules: *"Quod licet Jovi, non licet bovi?"* Politics seems to have gained ground on economics, for how long, no one knows, of course. The dilemma of how to benefit from trade with the West and yet at the same time slow down or even reverse economic reforms, if that trade becomes "dangerous," remains unresolved and is another important topic for further exploration, as is the Western problem of how to trade with the communist states without making unilateral concessions.

IV

Finally, all these actual or potential changes in East European countries (and elsewhere, too) occurring autonomously in their internal economies or induced by external events—and the realization that one academic discipline cannot be of great help in understanding societies which politicize economies to the extreme—have given or intensified *the impetus to look at economic systems in a more eclectic way*, going beyond one's discipline and expanding the framework of comparisons beyond communist (or Socialist) systems. This gives rise, for example, to the controversy about convergence.[29]

This complicates, of course, the problematics of classifying the economic systems of the individual East European states, because that requires not only clearly defined criteria of comparison but also distinctions between theoretical models and operational varieties, which is an arduous task. Even if traditional typologies are preserved and retested, the characterization of the reform blueprints and/or their implementation in relation to "market socialism" is not less complicated, because this "model" has its own theoretical varieties and operational gaps.[30]

Consequently, whether we have "within-system changes" or structural and functional "transformations" in Eastern Europe is a problem that depends to a considerable degree on the criteria and definitions adopted by the analyst, and on his reading of the various reforms.

However, regardless of the interpretations of the traditional market vs. command approach and its variations, there is little disagreement that Yugoslavia is at the one end, Hungary and Czechoslovakia (before August 1968) in the middle, and the rest at the other end of the reformist spectrum. Nor do many dispute the primacy of command elements in most of these economies.[31]

The new and different approach, noticeable since the late 1960s, is to expand the scope of comparisons and to involve a mix of ideological, political, as well as economic criteria. Zinam has provided the broadest framework in an attempt to devise a general theory of comparative economies; Mesa-Lago has compared socialist systems globally, and Montias has suggested a taxonomy of Soviet-type economies.[32] The initial result is a seeming *potpourri* of basic assumptions, system traits, and variables, but—as in the case with all innovative ventures—the tentative character of the results is readily acknowledged and the road is opened for refinements and a possible synthesis.

What is important for us is to recognize that existing typologies are too rigid and restricted and that—however difficult—we should try to provide ways and means to better comprehend the complex-ities of social phenomena—be they termed systems of cultures—by cross-fertilization among academic disciplines, especially politics and economics, and by comparisons among related systems or cultures. The study of communist states in Eastern Europe is particularly suitable for comparative political economics, and the present volume hopefully offers some food for thought.

Notes

1. Cf. the above chapters by Nove, Dellin, and Sik.

2. On the discussion phase, cf., *inter alia*, Eugene Zaleski, *Planning Reforms in the Soviet Union, 1962-1966* (Chapel Hill: University of North Carolina, 1967); George R. Feiwel, *The Soviet Quest for Economic Efficiency* (New York: Praeger, 1967); Myron E. Sharpe, ed., *The Liberman Discussion* (White Plains: IASP, 1965), and *Reform of Soviet Economic Management* (1966); and Michael Gamarnikow, *Economic Reforms in Eastern Europe* (Detroit: Wayne State University, 1968).

3. The Soviet reforms decreed in May and September 1965 can serve as an illustration of the divergence between private proposals and official blueprints. (Cf., e.g., Liberman's article in *Pravda*, Sept. 9, 1962, with Premier Kosygin's Report, ibid., Sept. 28, 1965, and with analytical comments in sources cited under note 2, as well as in Karl C. Thalheim and Hans-Hermann Hoehmann, eds., *Wirtschafts-reformen in Osteurope* (Economic Reforms in Eastern Europe) (Cologne: Wissenschaft und Politik, 1968).

4. Cf. Ota Sik's many writings, the latest of which are *Fakten ueber die tschechoslowakische Wirtschaft* (Facts on the Czechoslovak Economy) (Vienna: Molden, 1969) and *Der Strukturwandel der Wirtschaftssysteme in den osteuropaeischen Laenden* (The Changing Structure of the Economic Systems in the East European Countries) (Zurich: Arche Nova, 1971).

5. Many Soviet sources have been saying since 1968 that—to quote from *Voprosy ekonomiky*, no. 4, 1969—"contrary to the concept of the bourgeois scientists, the main task of the reform is not to weaken but to strengthen central planning." At the 1971 Party Congress, Kosygin himself stated that "directive planning" was the Soviet "leading and decisive principle." He emphasized: "Obviously, we reject all the various erroneous ideas that would replace the leading role of the state's central planning by market forces" (*Pravda*, April 2, 1971). Similar "reassurances" have been made by the Bulgarian leadership since 1968, after a reversal to central planning took place (see the chapter on Bulgaria). Excellent recent interpretative articles on the Soviet reforms are Gertrude E. Schroeder, "Soviet Economic Reforms: A Study in Contradiction," *Soviet Studies*, July 1968, and "Soviet Economic Reform at an Impasse," *Problems of Communism*, July-August 1971, as well as Gregory Grossman, "From the Eighth to the Ninth Five-Year Plan," in N.T. Dodge, ed., *24th Party Congress and 9th Five-Year Plan: Proceedings* (Mechanicsville, Maryland: Cremona, 1971).

6. For recent comments, see Michael Gamarnikow, "The Polish Economy in Transition," *Problems of Communism*, January-February 1970, and Harry Trend, "Analysis of Polish Economic Policies for 1971-1975 and Beyond," *Radio Free Europe Research*, December 13, 1971. The renewed attempt at reform is illustrated by the "Guidelines," adopted by the Plenum of the Central Committee on Sept. 4, 1971 and submitted to the Sixth Congress in December 1971, which, however, failed to pass any resolutions on the reform. (*Trybuna Ludu*, Dec. 7-12, 1971).

7. Cf. Deutsches Institut fuer Wirtschaftsforschung, *DDR– Wirtschaft* (CDR's Economy) (Frankfurt: Fischer, 1971), and the *Proceedings of the Eighth Party Congress* in June 1971 (*Information Bulletin*, nos. 16-17, 1971).

8. In Rumania, even the limited reform of 1967, originally designed to be fully implemented by the end of 1969, has been postponed, and Ceausescu has disclaimed any desire to relax the party's grip on the economy. (*Scanteia*, May 8, 1971).

Albania seems to be using the term "economic reform" to mean a more efficient centralization (see *Rruga e Partise*, October

1969, as cited in *Radio Free Europe Research*, November 3, 1969), and Hoxha's report to the 6th Party Congress in November 1971 (*Zeri i popullit*, Nov. 2, 1971).

9. Cf. Prime Minister Fock's speech on Oct. 22, 1971, discussing the current state of the new economic mechanism, *Népszabadsag*, Oct. 23, 1971, and Julius Zala, ibid., Oct. 24, 1971. Basic Hungarian works in English are Istvan Friss, ed., *Reform of the Economic Mechanism in Hungary* (Budapest, 1969) and articles in the Budapest *The New Hungarian Quarterly* (most notably by Jozsef Bognar, Rezso Nyers, Bela Sulyok, and Egon Kemenes). Among the growing literature on Hungary are recent articles by Richard D. Portes, "Economic Reforms in Hungary," AEA Proceedings, May 1970 and Harry G. Shaffer, "Progress in Hungary," *Problems of Communism*, January-February 1970, and Willy Linder's series "Ungarns Reformpolitiker auf neuen Wegen" (Hungary's Reformers Take New Paths), *Neue Zuercher Zeitung*, December 7, 13, 1969, and January 3, 6, and 9, 1970.

10. An excellent essay is Michael B. Petrovich, "Significance of the Yugoslav' Heresy," in R.V. Burks, ed., *The Future of Communism in Europe* (Detroit: Wayne State U. Press, 1968). See also Jaroslav Vanek, *The General Theory of Labor-Managed Market Economies* (Ithaca: Cornell U., 1970) and Egon Neuberger, "The Yugoslav Visible Hand System," in *Working Paper No. 3* (Bloomington: Indiana U., 1971). Among recent assessments by European authors, see Aleksander Bajt, "Decentralized Decision-Making Structure in the Yugoslav Economy," *Economics of Planning*, July 1967 and "Jugoslawiens Wirtschaftslage" (Yugoslavia's Economic Situation), *Wissenschaftlicher Dienst Suedosteuropa*, Nov. 1971. The 1971 nationality crisis, reflected also in the economic field, led to the enactment of an "Action Program" in January 1972 (*Komunist*, Jan. 29, 1972), which reconfirms that reform commitment, albeit within a recentralized political leadership.

11. It so happens that almost all of the communist parties of the area had their Congresses in 1971, thereby bringing us up to date on the comparative directions of their reforms.

12. Since this was written, disagreement between Budapest and Moscow was voiced in *Pravda* (Feb. 3, 1972), which made specific reference to "a greater need for the struggle against various manifestations of nationalist ideology." (Cf. *The New York Times*, April 9 and 12, 1972.

13. By "meaningful reform" I understand—along with Francesco Vito, "Decentralization in a Collectivist Planned Economy," in Jan S. Prybyla, ed., *Comparative Economic Systems* (New York: Apple-

ton-Century-Crofts, 1969), and W. Brus, "Problems of Decentralization in a Socialist Planned Economy," a paper prepared at the I.P.S.A. Round Table, Oxford, September 1963—decentralization "in the economic (not simply in the administrative or technical) sense," and a price system aimed at reflecting relative scarcities, i.e., a substantive modification of the command economy.

14. See the excellent essay by Gregory Grossman "Economic Reforms: The Interplay of Economics and Politics," in R.V. Burks, op. cit.

15. What "1984" will bring is anybody's guess, but I join those, like Nove, who feel that "the system has an inner logic that defies gradual change" (see his chapter herein) and that, therefore, reforms will materialize only if another debacle of the Soviet economy, more serious than in the early 1960s, makes the necessity for reforms amply clear to those who have the power to implement them.

16. This subject was discussed at another international symposium on "Reforms and Foreign Economic Relations" held within the framework of the Sixth International Conference and attended by Hermann Gross, Michael Gamarnikow, H.-H. Hoehmann, Ernst Lederer, Johann Hawlowitsch, and L.A.D. Dellin. Their papers were published in Alfred Domes, ed., *Reformen und Dogmen in Osteuropa* (Reforms and Dogmas in Eastern Europe) (Cologne: Wissenschaft und Politik, 1971). Portions of the Epilogue have been drawn from my comments at those proceedings.

17. The contribution of exports to GNP varied from a high of about 40 percent for Hungary to a low of about 20 percent for Poland, while the Soviet share was only 5 percent; see *Mir sotsializma v zifrakh i faktakh, 1968* (The Socialist World in Numbers and Facts) (Moscow: 1969, p. 129).

18. See the English text of the Program in United Nations General Assembly, *Report of the Economic and Social Council*, A/C 2/272, November 17, 1971. For useful comments see Henry Schaefer, "The 25th Comecon Council Session and the Integration Program," *Radio Free Europe Research*, September 1, 1971, and Heinrich Machowski, "Towards Socialist Economic Integration in Eastern Europe" (paper presented at an international conference at Columbia University, Dec. 2, 1971). Comecon's share in each country's trade has varied from a high of 75 percent for Bulgaria to a low of 36 percent for Rumania (*Statistical Yearbook of the CMEA* (Comecon) *Countries*, Moscow, 1970, p. 254).

19. Unlike the Common Market, Comecon is dominated by a single large power, the Soviet Union, which is also the largest trading partner of all of the member-states. See a useful analysis by Cal

Clark, "Foreign Trade as an Indicator of Political Integration in the Soviet Bloc" *International Studies Quarterly*, vol. 15, no. 3, Sept. 1971.

20. Rumania's position has somewhat changed (see her belated participation in the Investment Bank), and this is due obviously to Soviet pressure, but the basic motivation of preserving as much as possible of the country's independence and freedom of action remains unaltered (cf. *Viata Economica*, Aug. 27, 1971, *Problems of Peace and Socialism*, Oct. 1971, and *Probleme Economice*, December 1971, pp. 20-27).

21. For the original Hungarian position, cf. Rezso Nyers in *Nepszabadsag*, Jan. 23, 1969, and his interview in *Hospodarske Noviny*, July 25, 1969; also, Bela Csikos-Nagy in *Kosgazdasagi Szemle*, February, 1969, and the then Finance Minister Valyi in *Magyar Hirlap*, July 3, 1969. Typical recent examples of this maneuvering are the lead article in *Nepszabadsag*, July 26, 1970, and Valyi's interview in *Tarsadalmi Szemle*, Aug.-Sept., 1971. (Valyi is now Hungary's representative to the Comecon).

22. Cf. the "Complex Program" cited supra, n. 18. Illustrative of the Soviet position are the articles by Professor Oleg Bogomolov, the hard-line academician, who refutes the suggestion that improvements in the market mechanism are a necessary prerequisite for the integration process (see his "Economic Integration of the Socialist Countries," *World Marxist Review* no. 11, 1970 and *Problems of Peace and Socialism*, October, 1971).

23. For some recent Western analyses, see Alan A. Brown and Egon Neuberger, eds., *International Trade and Central Planning* (Berkeley: California University Press, 1968); P.J.D. Wiles, *Communist International Economics* (Oxford: Blackwell, 1968); and J.M. Montias, "Obstacles to the Economic Integration of Eastern Europe," *Studies in Comparative Communism*, July-October, 1969.

24. I have elaborated on this aspect in my "Political Factors in East-West Trade," *East Europe*, October 1969. GATT membership was obtained by Yugoslavia, Poland, and Rumania, and Hungary's application is pending. Requirements for Rumania's entry were lowered, which may ease the entry of other communist states. It is interesting to note that even Czechoslovakia, after years of self-imposed isolation, seems to be ready to vie for Western credits (see Bank Director S. Potac in *Finance a Uver*, Feb. 1972, pp. 73-81).

25. Such changes include the U.S. relaxation of trade barriers, which did not include the granting of MFN-status (except for Poland). The U.S. Congress enacted the Export Administration Act of 1969, decontrolling previously embargoed items and expanding

the credit-granting authority of the Export-Import Bank. On the communist attitudes, including their own non-recognition of the Common Market, see Henry W. Schaefer, "Kommunistische 'West-poltik' und die EWG" (Communist Policy Toward the West and How it Affects the Common Market), *Osteuropaeische Rundschau*, nos. 2 and 3, 1971, and his "Osteuropa und das GATT," (East Europe and the GATT) ibid., no. 2, 1972. It is interesting to read that there seems to be a communist "inferiority complex" vis-a-vis the Common Market where the future is concerned. Thus, as a communist source indicates, "it is not impossible that Western Europe will, as in the past, outpace the Comecon countries in the general level of industrial output and in other indices; at the end of the 1970s, the U.S. and Canada will still be in first place, with Japan in fourth" (*Politicheski Dnevnik*, no. 72, 1970, p. 6).

26. For some Western analysis, see the paper by Alec Nove on "East-West Trade," and comments thereon by J. Benard, Evsey D. Domar, Michael Kaiser, and John M. Montias, presented at the Congress of the International Economic Association, Montreal, September 2-7, 1968; also J. Wilczynski, *The Economics and Politics of East-West Trade*, (New York: Macmillan Co., 1969), Andrea Boltho, *Foreign Trade Criteria in Socialist Economies* (Cambridge: Univ. Press 1971); A.A. Brown and P. Marer, "East-West Trade, Old Issues and New Prospects," in U.S. Congress, Joint Economic Committee, *A Foreign Economic Policy for the 1970's* (Wash., D.C., 1971), pp. 1211-1226, and C.F.G. Ransom, "Obstacles to the Liberalization of Relations between E.E.C. and Comecon," *Studies in Comparative Communism*, July-October, 1969. Also, in German, Jens Meier and Johann Hawlowitsch, eds., *Die Aussenwirtschaft Suedosteuropas* (Southern Europe's Foreign Commerce) (Cologne: Wissenschaft und Politik, 1970), and Hermann Gross, ed., *Probleme des Ost-West Handels* (Problems of East-West Trade) (Bonn: Atlantik Forum, 1971). For some Eastern viewpoints, see D. Andreyev and M. Markov, "The Common Market after Eleven Years," *International Affairs*, January, 1969; Imre Vajda's paper presented at the International Congress, cited supra; and Soviet Foreign Trade Minister N. Patolichev in *Izvestiya*, Dec. 11, 1969.

27. Cf. the report by Andreas Adahl on "East-West Industrial Cooperation" to the Round Table Conference of the European League for Economic Cooperation in Brussels in December 1969. In Rumania, a new law on international cooperation was enacted on March 17, 1971 granting some limited freedom to foreign trade enterprises and opening the way for foreign investment, even in conjunction with Western firms (*Neuer Weg*, March 19, 1971). Hungary enacted a similar law on August 7, 1970.

28. On Yugoslavia, see Johann Hawlowitsch, "Jugoslawien" (Yugoslavia), in J. Meier and J. Hawlowitsch, eds., op. cit. The foreign investment act of 1967 was to be changed, permitting foreigners to repatriate their profits and also to hold a majority ownership in mixed enterprises (*New York Times*, Dec. 25, 1971 and January 1, 1972).

29. Pioneering in favor of the convergence thesis has been the group headed by Jan Tinbergen at the Dutch Economic Institute in Rotterdam. See his "Do Communist and Free Economies Show a Converging Pattern?", *Soviet Studies*, vol. 12, April 1961; also H. Linneman, J.P. Pronk, and J. Tinbergen, "Convergence of Economic Systems in the East and West," in Emile Benoit, ed., *Disarmament and World Economic Interdependence* (Oslo, 1967).

Opponents include J. S. Prybyla, see his "The Convergence of Western and Communist Economic Systems," *The Russian Review*, January 1964, and K.C. Thalheim, "Liberalisierungstendenzen im Ostblock?" (Liberalization Tendencies in Eastern Europe?), in B. Gleize, K.C. Thalheim, K.P. Hensel, and R. Meimberg, eds., *Der Osten auf dem Wege zur Marktwirtschaft* (The East on the Road to a Market Economy) (Berlin, 1967).

30. Suffice it to refer to the difference between Oskar Lange and Fred M. Taylor, on the one hand, and Abba P. Lerner, on the other. Recent contributions to the problematics are Benjamin N. Ward, *The Socialist Economy* (New York: Random House, 1967); Abram Bergson, "Market Socialism Revisited," *The Journal of Political Economy*, vol. 75, no. 5, October 1967; Francesco Vito, op. cit. and Jan S. Prybyla, "Meaning and Classification of Economic Systems," in Jan S. Prybyla, ed., op. cit.

31. Thalheim uses the terms "conservatives," "compromisers," and "progressives" (see his "Conclusion"). That the Soviet reforms do not constitute a "sufficient departure . . . of the command economy to really solve the ills that prompted the reforms" (Robert W. Campbell, "Economic Reforms in the USSR," *American Economic Review*, May, 1968) is widely agreed upon. It is also generally agreed that "with the exception of Yugoslavia, the countries of Eastern Europe have all retained *important* (italics supplied) elements of the command economy." (John M. Montias, "East European Economic Reforms," U.S. Senate, Committee on the Judiciary, *Hearings on Economic Concentration*, Washington, D.C., 1968).

32. Cf. Oleg Zinam, "The Economics of Command Economies," in Jan S. Prybyla, ed., *Comparative Economic Systems* (New York: Appleton-Century-Crofts, 1969); Carmelo Mesa-Lago, "A Continuum Model To Compare Socialist Systems Globally," paper presented at

the Northeastern Slavic Conference of the University of Vermont in April 1972, to be published in *Economic Development and Cultural Change* (Fall, 1972); and John M. Montias, "Types of Communist Economic Systems," in Chalmers Johnson, ed., *Change in Communist Systems* (Stanford: University Press, 1970).

About the Contributors

L.A.D. Dellin holds joint appointments as professor of economics and of political science at the University of Vermont and is director of its Center for Area and International Studies. He specializes in comparative communist systems and has been a Fulbright Research Scholar abroad. He is on the editorial board of several journals and a frequent consultant to the U.S. government. His publications include *Bulgaria* (1957) and essays and articles on East European economics and politics.

Michael Gamarnikow, a graduate of the Universities of Glasgow and London, is the author of *Economic Reforms in Eastern Europe* (1968) and of many essays and numerous articles on Eastern Europe. He was Senior Research Fellow at the Institute on Communist Affairs of Columbia University (1967-68).

Hermann Gross, Professor Economics and director of the Institute of the Economy and Society of Southeastern Europe at the University of Munich, with a joint appointment at the Munich School of Political Science, is one of the pioneers of East European studies, having taught at the Universities of Kiel, Leipzig, and Vienna in the inter-war period. A prolific writer and editor—his latest publication is *Probleme des Ost-West-Handels* (Problems of East-West Trade) (1971)—he specializes in international trade policy and is on the boards of many national and international journals and organizations.

Johann Hawlowitsch is a member of the Institute for the Economy and Society of Southeastern Europe at the University of Munich and specializes in Yugoslav economics. He has published many articles in German and English and represents the younger generation of German scholars.

Willy Linder, currently economics editor of the Swiss *Neue Züercher Zeitung* covers economic developments in Eastern Europe and especially in Hungary. He has written extensively on economic reforms for his newspaper as well as for many scholarly publications and holds a teaching position at the University of Zurich.

Alec Nove, one of the foremost authorities on the U.S.S.R., is Professor of Economics and director of the Institute of Soviet and East European Studies at the University of Glasgow. He is the author of a standard text, *The Soviet Economy* (currently in its third revised edition), *Was Stalin Really Necessary?* (1964), and of many other publications, both technical and popular. He is also the chairman of the editorial board of the prestigious British quarterly *Soviet Studies.*

Claus D. Rohleder, a member of the Institute for the Economy and Society of Southeastern Europe at the University of Munich, specializes in Rumania and East-West trade. Among his publications is *Die Osthandelspolitik der EWG-Mitgliedstaaten, Grossbritanniens und der USA gegenueber den Staatshandelslaendern Suedosteuropas* (Trade Policies of the Common Market Countries, Great Britain, and the USA toward the State-Trading Countries of Southeast Europe) (1969).

Ota Sik, whose name is inexorably connected with the economic reform movement in Czechoslovakia, was Deputy Prime Minister in A. Dubcek's government during the "Prague Spring" and head of the government commission on economic reforms from 1963-68. Exiled in Switzerland, he is currently Adjunct Professor of Economics at the University of St. Gallen. Among his many writings are *Plan and Market Under Socialism* (1967) and *Der Strukturwandel der Wirtschaftssysteme in den osteuropaeischen Laendern* (Structural Change in East European Economic Systems) (1971).

Karl C. Thalheim, Professor of Economics and director of the Economics Section of the Institute on East Europe at the Free University of Berlin, is one of the pioneers of Soviet and East European studies, specializing in comparative systems and the Soviet and Central European economies in particular. Among his scores of publications are *Die Wirtschaft der Sowjetzone in Krise und Umbau* (The Soviet Zone-East German Economy in Crisis and Reconstruction) (1964) and, in co-editorship, *Wirschaftsreformen in Osteuropa* (Economic Reforms in Eastern Europe) (1968). He is also editor of a series of monographs on East Europe published by the Berlin Institute.

Index